CW00869301

LEGENDARY TRIALS

BY
DANIEL J. LANAHAN J.D.

authorHOUSE®

AuthorHouse™
1663 Liberty Drive
Bloomington, IN 47403
www.authorhouse.com
Phone: 1 (800) 839-8640

© *2019 Daniel J. Lanahan J.D. All rights reserved.*

No part of this book may be reproduced, stored in a retrieval system, or transmitted by any means without the written permission of the author.

Published by AuthorHouse 03/29/2019

ISBN: 978-1-7283-0224-9 (sc)
ISBN: 978-1-7283-0225-6 (hc)
ISBN: 978-1-7283-0223-2 (e)

Print information available on the last page.

Any people depicted in stock imagery provided by Getty Images are models, and such images are being used for illustrative purposes only. Certain stock imagery © *Getty Images.*

This book is printed on acid-free paper.

Because of the dynamic nature of the Internet, any web addresses or links contained in this book may have changed since publication and may no longer be valid. The views expressed in this work are solely those of the author and do not necessarily reflect the views of the publisher, and the publisher hereby disclaims any responsibility for them.

INTRODUCTION

IN AN OPENING STATEMENT, a trial lawyer intends to provide a verbal roadmap as to what he or she believes the evidence produced will show or prove. As in many human endeavors, the evidence is not always clear and direct.

In the following chapters, I wish to show that while our society has advanced greatly in the areas of science, transportation, conveniences and yes, even war, we as human beings continue to view our affairs in a very personal and judgmental way. Although the law has changed, expanded and become more complex, the issues tend to remain the same. Have we learned from our experiences over the last one hundred plus years or do we keep arguing the same issues, in the same manner with the same result? No progression, no learning, no advancement of new ideas, always hoping for a different result. Someone once suggested this was a prescription for lunacy, but in reality it is just we humans going over the same ground purporting to be enlightened, but are we? Compare cases from many years ago with those that are more familiar and those reported by the popular media in the last 20 years. Determine if how we approach our affairs from a public perception point of view based on our personal views has in fact created a society that has addressed and improved its human discourse in any appreciable way or whether it is the same old/same old or worse.

Being a lawyer interested in history, it is my belief a non-scholarly but factual and easily readable summary of famous trials helps one to understand the societal issues, legal principles and historical significance of the events that led to the judicial resolution of notorious cases at the time they took place. Some issues raised generations ago remain with us and in some minds many are unresolved. Knowledge of past events is instructive in dealing with similar issues we presently face. Finally, some of these real life stories are just plain interesting reading. They may help us remember events we were alive to witness and place them in context or learn anew about cases of which we only have vague knowledge. Use of the words "black" or "blacks" in the Civil Rights cases were words appropriate for those times. Now, I prefer the use of the term African-Americans. I wish you well as you pass through the last 100 years plus with occasional relevant flashbacks added for the purpose of contrast. One may ask why certain other cases have not been dealt with. The answer often is the author, while acknowledging some trials not mentioned were notorious, believes they lack historical significance. That is the case of O.J. Simpson. While notorious it is not particularly instructive and because it received so much publicity repetition is not necessary. One might consider this case when reading the case of Lizzie Borden. Except for race and gender there are similarities.

I have selected specific cases involving real people during specific periods of our history to demonstrate "what goes around comes around". If the reader gains no more insight than just learning about interesting stories, I have accomplished my goal. If, on the other hand, it results in new thought, I have exceeded my highest expectations.

Daniel J. Lanahan
Puerto Vallarta
March 2019

TABLE OF CONTENTS

CHAPTER 1

COMMONWEALTH OF MASSACHUSETTS v. LIZZIE A. BORDEN

IT WAS HOT AND humid in the spring and early summer of 1893 in New Bedford, Bristol County, Massachusetts. Chief Justice Albert Mason with Associate Justices Caleb Blodgett and Justin Dewey were preparing for the trial of Lizzie A. Borden. The profile of defendant Borden, including the fact she was a middle class caucasian and the hideous nature of the crime, created vast publicity. District Attorney Hosea M. Knowlton with the help of his assistant, William H. Moody, was also preparing. He had the burden to prove beyond a reasonable doubt the truth of the Grand Jury indictment of December 2, 1892 alleging Lizzie Andrew Borden of Fall River, Massachusetts, murdered her step-mother, Abby Durfee Borden and her father, Andrew Jackson Borden, on August 4, 1892 by assaulting both decedents with sharp, cutting instruments.

George D. Robinson, Andrew J. Jennings, and Melvin O. Adams were preparing the defense of Ms. Borden whose inconsistent statements to the police and others, as well as her Grand Jury testimony resulted in the indictment. At the time, none of the participants knew the trial would result in a controversy that would be discussed, analyzed and

1

replayed hundreds of times over the ensuing 100-plus years. When the trial began on June 5, 1893, the public packed the area around the New Bedford courthouse and they stayed until it concluded on June 20, 1893. Obviously, public perception of guilt or innocence affected the result in this case.

Trials that receive massive publicity are no doubt subject to the possibility and perhaps, on occasion, the probability the result will be affected. Potential jurors, notwithstanding their being questioned before selection (voir dire), are subject to public opinion. They are human beings and generally arrive at the courthouse with perceptions formed by the information received prior to the trial. Experienced trial attorneys do not try to totally change a juror's mind during a trial. Instead they play to and reinforce jurors' prior perceptions. It is very difficult to completely change a person's perceptions unless they are weak-minded. An analogy of this technique would be military intelligence trying to plant the perception in an enemy's mind that certain events will occur when in fact plans call for a completely different scenario.

During World War II the allies created a mythical army under the command of General George Patton and had it stationed in southern England near the closest point to the coast of continental Europe. For a long time, Hitler had the perception that was where the allies would invade. Rather than attempt to deceive Hitler into believing the invasion would not be at Normandy, the allies chose to play to his belief that the invasion would be at Pas-de-Calais. The mythical army used radio broadcasts, as well as rubber artillery, tanks and trucks which when photographed by the German Air Force, reinforced Hitler's preconceived idea of the invasion location. Trial attorneys must do the same with jurors, knowing most have preconceived ideas when they arrive in the courtroom. Their strategy is to support and reinforce the jurors' preconceived ideas or perceptions rather than convince them they are wrong. The art of jury selection is ascertaining those preconceived preconceptions.

Lizzie Andrew Borden, age 32 at the time of the murders, lived with her sister Emma, ten years her senior, her stepmother, Abby, age 64, and her father, Andrew, age 70, at 92 Second Street, Fall River, Massachusetts in a two story wooden house a short distance from the center of the town. The only other regular occupant of the four bedroom house was their maid, Bridget (Maggie) Sullivan, a 26 year old unmarried Irish woman, residing in a small room in the attic. On the day before the murders, Lizzie's uncle, John V. Moss, the brother of Lizzie's natural mother who had passed away when she was a young child, came to visit. He stayed in the fourth bedroom, the guestroom, where stepmother Abby Borden was subsequently found murdered.

The house was divided so there was no access between the second floor bedroom of Mr. and Mrs. Borden, reached only by a rear staircase from the first floor, and the bedrooms occupied by Lizzie and Emma. These rooms were accessed from a front staircase on the first floor which also served as the only entrance to the guestroom. At one time the second floor was open for passage, however doors were kept locked with furniture placed in front of them so as to create the separation.

Medical and other evidence indicate Mrs. Borden was murdered at approximately 9:30 a.m. on August 4, 1892. The evidence also shows Mr. Borden was murdered approximately one hour and a half later while he was lounging on a couch in the first floor sitting room. During the trial, numerous highly qualified physicians testified regarding the times of the deaths determined by the temperature of the bodies and the defense did not attempt to dispute this evidence.

A popular diddy at the time went as follows:
Lizzie Borden took an axe,
And gave her mother 40 whacks,
When she saw what she had done, She gave her father 41.

In fact, 29 blows were struck with an axe to the heads of the decedents. Mr. Borden received 11 blows and Mrs. Borden 18, all to the face and head. In both cases the first blow, which was from behind, was fatal. The remaining blows were frontal so the faces of the victims were barely recognizable. The medical testimony stated the blows were caused by an axe or a hatchet, a number of which were found in and around the house. At the time tools such as these were commonplace but none in the Borden household showed blood stains.

In any crime, especially murder, police consider three elements to determine an individual suspect. They are motive, means, and opportunity. Within a short time Lizzie became the only suspect although popular opinion held a deranged, wild individual must have been the killer because the acts were so ferocious. Although the maid had opportunity, since only she along with Lizzie were in the house at the time of the murders, no motive could be ascertained. The uncle was away visiting friends and had an excellent alibi. At the time of the murder of Mrs. Borden, Mr. Borden had taken a walk downtown and was seen and spoken to by a number of people. Because of his whereabouts and since he was murdered in the same manner, he was never considered a suspect in the death of his wife. The sister, Emma, was away visiting friends in Fairhaven, a town approximately 15 miles away and had been away for a few days before the murders. Investigators quickly zeroed in on Lizzie because she seemed to be the only one, other than the maid, with opportunity and she gave conflicting statements to the police regarding her whereabouts at the time the murders.

When interviewed shortly after the murders, Lizzie told the police her mother had been called away because she received a note indicating someone was ill. Allegedly she left the house about 9:00 a.m., and Lizzie never saw her again until her body was found. The note was never discovered. Despite a reward being posted for information regarding the sick person she might have visited, no information was forthcoming. Lizzie later indicated she thought she heard her mother return, but did not see or speak with her. At approximately 9:30 a.m., Mr. Borden returned from his walk downtown and because all the doors were locked, he had to be let in the front door by the maid. Maggie testified that as she let Mr. Borden into the house at the front door she heard a noise that sounded like someone laughing. She looked up and saw Lizzie standing at the top of the front staircase. Lizzie was approximately 20 feet from the location of Mrs. Borden's body which was later found on the floor in the guestroom. The maid testified that Lizzie then came down the staircase and helped her father who was not feeling well, perhaps because of the heat, lie down on the couch in the living room. The maid then went about her business cleaning the windows on the outside of the house and Lizzie did some ironing.

Later that afternoon Lizzie told a neighbor and the police different stories as to what she did between the time her father came home and discovering his body at approximately 11:00 a.m. She told a neighbor, Mrs. Russell, she had gone to the barn to get a piece of iron to fix a window. Shortly thereafter she told a police officer, and in fact repeated this story on a number of occasions including under oath at an inquest, that she had gone to the barn and went up to the loft to find some lead with which to make sinkers because she intended to go fishing the following week. She stated she was in the barn mostly in the loft for approximately 20 minutes before the discovery of Mr. Borden's body. An investigating police officer looked over the loft floor and saw no disturbance of hay dust, noted it was extremely hot because of the temperature and that the loft window was closed. From his testimony it was clear he found no evidence anyone had been in the hayloft. While it is true Lizzie planned on going fishing, her story regarding needing sinkers was highly suspect because she had not seen or touched her fishing equipment, which was located at a farm owned by her father, for over five years and could not testify whether or not in fact there were sinkers with the equipment.

At the scene after the father's body was found, Lizzie seemed to be the only one not confused and seemingly as an afterthought suggested perhaps someone look for her stepmother who she thought might have come home. Only then did they find her body on the second floor in the guest bedroom.

Interesting legal issues arose because of Lizzie's testimony at an inquest held approximately ten days after the murders. She was subpoenaed to testify but was not allowed to have the family lawyer, Mr. Jennings, with her during her testimony even though she requested his presence. Prior to that, on August 6, 1892, immediately after the funeral, the mayor of Fall River, accompanied by the police chief, made a comment to her indicating she was a suspect. The Massachusetts Constitution, like the U.S. Constitution, has a clause that states no person shall be compelled to be a witness against himself. Because she was subpoenaed and therefore compelled to testify, her attorneys filed a motion with the three justices to preclude admission of her inquest testimony. The prosecution wanted this testimony introduced into evidence because it contained, what they thought to be, numerous inconsistencies and therefore, would be helpful to their case. Of course the defense wanted it excluded for the same reason.

This occurred long before the United States Supreme Court Miranda decision in the 1960's, and the only legal argument that applied was based on the fact the testimony was not voluntary. Even at that time involuntary statements were excluded, however, it was not clear that a subpoena was compulsion to the extent the testimony rendered would be involuntary. She could have raised her right against self-incrimination and not testified although that, of course, would give rise to a perception of guilt. The justices decided her testimony was improperly compelled and therefore it was not admitted into evidence, dealing a blow to the prosecution.

Based on her inconsistent statements, the prosecution advanced a "consciousness of guilt" theory in addition to the very specific evidence Lizzie Borden tried to buy prussic acid on the day before the murders. Not only was she known by the pharmacist but also by two other customers in the pharmacy who overheard the conversation wherein she requested the acid in order to clean a seal skin cape. The pharmacist told her she needed a prescription which she did not have and refused to sell it to her. Again, three justices on a motion to exclude this evidence ruled in favor of the defendant simply stating there was no evidence she had successfully purchased the prussic acid, and therefore the offered evidence was not relevant to any issue in the case. One element was certainly premeditation and most legal scholars who have reviewed this issue question the decision to exclude this evidence. Perhaps if the Justices had based their decision on the fact the evidence was extremely prejudicial, especially since the decedents were not poisoned, their decision would be considered more reasonable. There was evidence that a few days before the murders both Mr. and Mrs. Borden were quite ill and in fact Lizzie stated she was also ill and had vomited although there was no evidence, except her testimony, to that effect. Mr. and Mrs. Borden did see their family physician who thought that perhaps something might have been wrong with their milk and that they suffered from food poisoning. On the day before the murders, Lizzie visited a friend and told her she was concerned for the safety of her family because someone may have tried to poison them and also because their barn had been broken into on two occasions during the preceding year. The friend pointed out the break-ins were by young boys looking for rodents and that it was very unlikely anyone would poison their milk which was delivered very early in the morning and therefore would have to be tampered with in daylight.

The prosecution also had to prove motive and this was not particularly difficult. Up until five years before the murders, Lizzie and her stepmother got along very well and in fact Lizzie called her mother. However, because Lizzie's father had given some property to her stepmother's sister, Lizzie and Emma both became annoyed and thought their inheritance was being dissipated. Mr. Borden, a very successful banker, had accumulated a fair amount of wealth. He owned two farms and other real estate. Thereafter the two sisters' relationship with their stepmother was strained. They rarely ate meals as a family and although they would occasionally talk, Lizzie would always call her stepmother Mrs. Borden. There was some indication Mr. Borden had decided to make a will shortly before his death, however that was never proven.

The prosecution proved Lizzie had a strained relationship with her stepmother and father; she had opportunity since she was in the house at the time of both murders; and she had means which was the use of one or more of the axes found on the property. What was not properly explained was how she could have committed both murders and not have even a single blood splatter on her dress. Not only did she have to clean the ax or axes she used but also change her dress before finding her father's body. She had time to do this. The only evidence hinting of any of this was vague testimony that on August 7, 1892 she burned a dress. The only person alive to testify regarding what Lizzie was wearing on the morning of the murders, other than Lizzie herself, was the maid and she could not remember with any particularity the dress Lizzie wore before the bodies were found.

In summary, the entire case against Lizzie Borden was based on circumstantial evidence. However, it was strong evidence and to believe her not guilty one had to envision an intruder who somehow got into the locked house, perhaps through a back door which the maid had failed to latch. This person would then have to remain hidden in the house, after murdering Mrs. Borden, for approximately one hour and a half before murdering Mr. Borden notwithstanding the fact Lizzie and the maid, also in the house, did not see any such intruder. Nevertheless, at that time the New England jury was not able to conclude a churchgoing woman of puritan blood could commit such hideous crimes. She was found not guilty in approximately one hour by the all male jury.

Just a few years before these murders, a woman named Sarah Jane Robinson had been convicted in Massachusetts of killing seven people although her murders were committed with poison which was much more typical of the means used by female murderers. There was little or no precedence for a well bred woman of high standards to be an axe murderer. After her acquittal, Lizzie and Emma stayed in Fall River until Emma moved to New Hampshire in approximately 1905. In the early 1920's, the two sisters were in litigation against each other over property issues but the case was never brought to trial. In June of 1927, Lizzie died at Fall River and Emma died at New Market, New Hampshire a short time later.

Although Lizzie Borden was found not guilty of the murders of her stepmother and father, the historical truth may well be different.

Because important evidence was excluded, the jury may well have had a reasonable doubt as to her guilt, however the rulings excluding the offered evidence are themselves suspect. Many legal writers have stated a general dissatisfaction with the law of evidence administered at the trial. Why were the judges and jurors swayed by the defendant or put another way, not persuaded by the prosecution? Could it be the fact that she was a religious woman with great support from church and community leaders? Could they not believe it was possible one of their own would commit such atrocious acts? Was it because she was a woman, and had the support of women's groups including those fighting for suffrage?

Finally, was it because New Englanders generally could not perceive and therefore were not prepared to accept the fact such a person could inflict extremely brutal wounds on a human being?

The next case which also took place in Massachusetts less than 30 years later highlights how perceptions developed by the time, place, other events surrounding the crime and the individuals involved, affected another jury decision.

CHAPTER 2

COMMONWEALTH OF MASSACHUSETTS V. NICOLA SACCO & BARTOLOMEO VANZETTI

AGAIN IT WAS LATE spring, early summer, but the year was 1920. The place was also Massachusetts, where Nicola Sacco and Bartolomeo Vanzetti were in jail awaiting trial. In the first of two trials Vanzetti was the only defendant and he was accused of assault with the intent to commit armed robbery. The prosecutor, District Attorney Frederick Katzmann, hoped to convict Vanzetti so that when he was subsequently tried, along with Sacco for a murder that occurred in another robbery, Vanzetti would have a record as a convicted felon. One reason for this tactic was the prosecution's generally weak case and the lack of evidence in the murder case against Vanzetti in particular.

During the early morning hours of December 24, 1919, it was alleged Bartolomeo Vanzetti and other unknown individuals, generally considered to be three or four in number, while in a Buick Touring car attempted to block the passage of a truck carrying the payroll of the White Shoe Company. Two of the robbers fired shots at the truck, whose occupants returned fire. The robbery was unsuccessful. The local Bridgewater Police Chief voiced the opinion that the criminals were anarchists, a number of whom had been drifting into the "Shoe" towns.

The second crime occurred in South Braintree, Massachusetts on April 15, 1920, at approximately 9:30 a.m. A payroll for the Slater and Morrall Shoe Co., was turned over by a representative of American Railway Express to a man named Parmenter, the company's paymaster and a guard named Berardelli. As the paymaster and guard left the Railway Express office, they passed two strangers leaning against a fence and were immediately fired upon. Berardelli dropped the money and fell. One of the robbers, later identified by a man named Pelser as Nicola Sacco, stood over the guard and shot four or five times into his body so that he died instantly. Parmenter ran but was also shot and killed. A Buick appeared and the murderers, now joined by a third individual, took the two metal boxes and fled in the car, firing as they went to deter pursuit. Newspapers connected the Bridgewater and South Braintree crimes.

It was discovered that just a few days before the attempted robbery at Bridgewater, which was thought to be committed by Italians or other foreigners, a Buick Touring car had been stolen from a Dr. Murphy. This car was found abandoned near Bridgewater just a few days after the murders at South Braintree, hence the police pursued Italians known to have a car. They learned a man named Mike Boda had taken his vehicle to a garage in West Bridgewater and they requested the garage owner notify them if someone came to pick it up. A number of men arrived at Johnson's Garage for the car, the police were tipped off, and subsequently Nicola Sacco and Bartolomeo Vanzetti, two of the five that had arrived, were detained and arrested since they were in possession of guns. The Press immediately published pictures of both defendants with accounts of the circumstances of their arrest including the claim of a police officer that they had tried to use their guns. This claim was untrue. Opinions were expressed they were probably connected with the Bridgewater and Braintree crimes.

Sacco had been employed by the Milfred Shoe Company and was married with children. When the 1917 Draft Law was passed he fled to Mexico to evade the draft but returned a few months later to be with his family. He worked for awhile under an assumed name. When the war ended, he resumed his identity and became employed at another shoe company in Stoughton, Massachusetts. He was a hard worker who did not miss work and therefore was considered steady. He had accumulated some savings. When arrested, after leaving the garage, he possessed a .32 caliber Colt pistol and Vanzetti a .38 caliber Harrington & Richardson revolver. Sacco had learned of his mother's death in Italy in early 1920 and had arranged to visit his father and so he had secured a passport. He was arrested just a few days before he was to sail.

Vanzetti arrived in New York in 1908. He worked at various odd jobs and ended up in Springfield Massachusetts working on the railroad. By 1913 he was in Plymouth and remained there until his arrest. Sometime in 1916 Sacco and Vanzetti met each other through membership in an anarchist group. Vanzetti also escaped to Mexico to avoid the draft in 1917. During the spring of 1920, friends of both Sacco and Vanzetti were being deported as a result of a crackdown by the United States Attorney General.

Eyewitnesses from the Braintree murders were asked to identify both defendants. Some could make no identification, others picked Sacco as one of the bandits who had done the shooting, and others identified Sacco as being near the crime scene or in the murderers' car after the crime. It was established that Sacco had been at work on December 24, 1919, and therefore he was never accused of being involved in the attempted robbery at Bridgewater. When first questioned regarding his activities on April 15, 1920, he stated he had been working. Later he claimed he was at the Italian Consulate in Boston getting his passport. Originally no one claimed to have observed Vanzetti at the murder scene.

Subsequently, witnesses stated Vanzetti was in the get away car hence he was charged. On the day of his arrest Vanzetti could not recall where he had been on April 15, the day of the murders. When asked about the Bridgewater attempted robbery on Christmas Eve, he did clearly remember delivering eels which were in great demand by the Italian community for Christmas. The defense produced credible documents to support this alibi. He also then remembered selling fish in Plymouth on April 15.

On June 11, 1920, indictments were brought against Vanzetti for assault with intent to rob and with intent to kill during the Bridgewater attempted truck hold-up. He was tried and convicted; hence he became a convicted felon which was used against him in the second trial wherein he, along with Sacco, were accused of the capital murders at South Braintree on April 15, 1920.

The second trial took place between May 31 and July 14, 1921, at Dedham, Massachusetts. The trial judge was again Webster Thayer who arguably was prejudiced against the defendants. He had already sentenced Vanzetti to 12 to 15 years for the attempted hold-up at Bridgewater, a heavy sentence considering no one was hurt and it was a failed crime. The Judge was also reported to have expressed intense dislike for "anarchists".

Both the prosecutor, Frederick Katzmann, and defense attorney, Frederick Moore, were aided by others. Moore, a California lawyer with radical connections, had acquired a reputation from successfully defending two other radicals on charges of murder arising out of a strike in Lawrence, Massachusetts. Except for that one case, Moore had no familiarity with court procedures in Massachusetts. He had been chosen by the radical group in charge of the defense and was not particularly liked by Sacco. Early on some of the defendants' friends had tried to replace Moore with well known local attorney William G. Thompson who, while he never took part in the trial, did attend the proceedings to become familiar with the matter. After the convictions, Moore was replaced by Thompson who represented the defendants thereafter.

Five hundred individuals were summoned as prospective jurors. The Judge questioned them in five areas: relationship to the defendants or decedents; interest in the result of the trial; formation of opinions; bias or prejudice; and ability to find the defendants guilty of a crime punishably by death.

In Massachusetts, the Judge voir dires the jury. He pointed out that mere impressions or light opinion based on news stories would not disqualify them. His instructions required only a willingness to dislodge such opinions if testimony reasonably demanded it. One juror, Ripley, volunteered he had been a client of the assistant prosecutor but he was allowed to remain and was, in fact, later named the foreman. After four days with only seven jurors selected, the panel was exhausted. A juror, Dolbeare, was excused because on the day of the murders he saw a fast moving automobile drive past him. Later he appeared as a witness against Vanzetti.

The Judge sent the Sheriff out to summon two hundred men for the next morning. These panelists, taken from their beds, social halls and work were not pleased when they arrived in court the next day. The defense objected since the manner of their selection was not random. A number of deputy sheriffs were questioned regarding how they selected the potential jurors. It was obvious many chosen were individuals the sheriffs knew and a large number of the two hundred were not selected arbitrarily but specifically chosen by the deputies. On June 6 the all male jury was selected. It included two machinists, a real estate dealer, a grocer, a stock keeper, a mason, mill workers, a photographer and a farmer.

Trial actually started on Tuesday June 7, 1921. The prosecution's case depended upon the following: (a) seven eyewitnesses' identification of Sacco as being present at or near the shooting; (b) one witness' identification of Sacco as being one of the murderers; (c) one of the bullets found in the body of Berardelli being fired by Sacco's pistol; (d) a hat found near the scene of the crime was Sacco's being identified as his by a former employer; (e) the revolver found on Vanzetti being taken by Sacco from Berardelli and given to Vanzetti; (f) Berardelli's gun being repaired shortly before the shooting and Vanzetti's weapon showing marks of similar repairs; and (g) the defendants' false alibis given shortly after their detention and arrest establishing a consciousness of wrong doing, i.e., a consciousness of guilt.

On Wednesday June 22, 1921, the 19th day of the trial, the defense gave its opening statement. It relied on the presumption of innocence, reasonable doubt based on the evidence and alibis supported by witnesses.

The defense produced numerous witnesses to testify neither of the defendants were present at or near the scene of the crime. They had more alibi witnesses than the prosecution's eyewitnesses. It is well known eyewitness testimony is often unreliable especially when the defendant is unknown to the witness.

Experts disputed the prosecution's evidence concerning the mortal bullet. Similarities between hats and revolvers were proved and the history of the gun found on Vanzetti was traced through prior ownership and it was not Berardelli's. Finally, to explain the charges of suspicious conduct by the defendants giving false information after their arrest, both defendants took the stand. This unfortunately resulted in the disclosure of their radical beliefs, supporting their claim that they feared deportation because of their anarchism (their motive for lying about their whereabouts at the time of the crimes) and not because of criminal activities.

After being found guilty of murder in the first degree, a motion for a new trial was made to Judge Thayer. With regard to the evidence concerning the fatal bullet being fired through Sacco's pistol the Judge pointed out a police officer testified for the prosecution even though rebutted by two defense experts. He found the jury had an opportunity to inspect the bullet using magnifying glasses and that they could compare the various marks themselves. This would never be allowed in a modern trial. Eyewitnesses identified Sacco as being "bare-headed" when he left the scene of the murder in the "bandit car." One of Sacco's prior employers testified the cap was similar to one Sacco hung on a nail next to his at work and that there were holes in the lining made as a result of how the cap was hung. Both Sacco and his wife testified that the cap was not his. The judge found the jury accepted the evidence that the cap was Sacco's.

The evidence against Vanzetti was minimal. Witnesses testified they had seen him in South Braintree or in nearby areas on April 15th. No one testified he was at the scene of the crime and the only physical evidence connecting him was the revolver seized at the time of his arrest. The prosecution argued it was the same revolver that belonged to the guard. However, subsequent review of the evidence long after the execution of the defendants showed the caliber of the weapon (.38) seized from Vanzetti at the time of his arrest was completely different than the one the guard owned (.32) although the manufacturer was the same. Vanzetti, taking the stand to explain the falsehoods told after his arrest, allowed the prosecution to impeach his credibility by using his conviction for the Bridgewater attempted robbery. Vanzetti, on crossexamination, admitted that he lied about the length of time he had known Sacco and explained he told that lie to hide the fact they had gone together to Mexico to avoid draft registration. One must question the defendants testifying on their own behalf as it is always a risky tactic. No doubt defense counsel felt the risk had to be taken.

Between their convictions in 1921 and their execution on August 23, 1927, appeals were taken to the Supreme Judicial Court of Massachusetts, petitions were filed with the Governor, a commission was appointed to investigate the convictions, a writ of habeas corpus was denied by the United States Supreme Court and the United States Circuit Court of Appeals, the latter occurring just three days before their execution. During the post-conviction and pre-execution years there were numerous demonstrations all over the world. The general consensus was that Sacco and Vanzetti were unjustly accused, tried with tampered and perjured evidence, and were being executed because they were immigrants, representing a new wave of society entering the United States, thereby threatening the peace of those already in the country.

Subsequent to the convictions, motions were brought charging Judge Thayer with prejudice. It was claimed he spoke with hostility against the defendants with his friends, on trains, at the University Club of Boston and at the golf club of Worchester, Massachusetts. It was alleged the Judge had made up his mind before the trial. Statements given to the governor of Massachusetts during clemency hearings supported the argument the Judge was hostile to defendants, the courtroom atmosphere was contentious and the Judge was belligerent towards the defense attorneys. Judge Thayer was a graduate of Dartmouth College (1879) and had been appointed a judge in 1917. At the time of the trial he was 74 years of age. He had experience trying civil and criminal trials in Norfolk, Plymouth, and neighboring counties. Perhaps the most explicit evidence of judge Thayer's bias was that given by Professor James P. Richardson of Dartmouth College, a conservative lawyer, who had known Judge Thayer for a long time. He testified regarding a conversation he had with Judge Thayer at the College wherein the Judge stated: "Did you see what I did with those anarchistic bastards the other day? I guess that will hold them for awhile." The witness had known Judge Thayer for approximately 15 years and was shocked at the comment. This witness also wrote the governor of Massachusetts supporting the appointment of an independent commission to study the trial and convictions. Governor Fuller did appoint a commission chaired by Harvard President A. Lawrence Lowell. It was filled out by Judge Robert Grant and Samuel W. Stratton. This commission, known as the Governor's Advisory Committee, concluded there was no reason to reverse the convictions or grant clemency.

On November 18, 1925, a man named Madeiros, also a prisoner at Dedham Prison, delivered a statement to Sacco stating he had been present during the murders at Braintree, although he himself had not fired the shots. He stated that as a youth of 18 he was persuaded to go with others without knowing where they were going or what was to be done, except that there was to be a holdup. Madeiros implicated the Morelli Gang of Providence, Rhode Island. Madeiros' statement, as are most convict statements, was not convincing.

Other information brought forth during post-trial hearings and clemency petitions included evidence from two individuals who stated that the prosecution's police weapons expert told them his real opinion was that the fatal bullet had not been fired through Sacco's pistol. Evidence was introduced that the police chief of Braintree, who testified about the tear in the cap found near the body of Beradelli, (the tear attributed to the cap being hung up on a nail) was in fact a rip made by the police chief when he attempted to find a name under the lining before he delivered the cap to the officers investigating the case.

Subsequent investigation by historians and interested parties certainly created reasonable doubt as to the guilt of Sacco and Vanzetti for the South Braintree murders. The case is particularly interesting legally because of the "consciousness of guilt" argument of the prosecution and by its apparent manipulation of the evidence without which there certainly would not have been sufficient evidence to bring the case to trial, much less obtain a conviction. It would be reasonable to conclude that using the "guilt beyond a reasonable doubt" standard the defendants would not have been found guilty if all of the evidence disclosed after their trial was considered. It certainly shows the power of a jury verdict and the unwillingness of higher authorities to overturn a jury's verdict even when there is substantial conflicting evidence. Again the verdict of history differs from that of the jury.

At the time of the events set forth in this case, there was civil unrest in many large eastern cities and the public was generally blaming that situation on immigrants who disagreed with the social order of the time and wanted to highlight the plight of the working man and woman. There were bombings and other acts of terrorism directed against government officials including judges. United States Attorney General Palmer had initiated what became known as the "Palmer raids" wherein government agents seized immigrants and rapidly deported them using methods many argued did not provide due process of law. The public assumed that if the defendants were arrested they were no doubt guilty and the media played to those perceptions.

Consider the more recent case of O.J. Simpson. He was a well respected star football player and many couldn't conceive he could commit a monstrous crime that spilled more blood than Lizzie Borden's ax. The defense played to that perception and tried the police. It worked, but probably only because the public generally couldn't believe such a popular individual could perpetrate such an atrocity. On the other hand, a subsequent civil jury found he probably committed the crime and found him liable. Possibly public perception changed in the period between the two trials, certainly the burden of proof was reduced and the police were not on trial in the civil suit.

Consider the recent case of Scott Peterson, wherein the public, despite early press indications that the prosecution case was weak, continued to believe his guilt. In fact when he was found guilty, cheering took place outside of the courthouse in Redwood City, California. The public follows notorious trials closely. It has been estimated one hundred million persons listened to the O.J. Simpson verdict on October 3, 1995. The popularity of Court TV and the TV show "America's Most Wanted" evidence the public's fascination with criminal trials.

There is no question media influences the public and the public influences jury trial results notwithstanding all of the protections our system of law provides. The public and the jurors are human and no matter how they try, perceptions form opinions and they stay with jurors in the courtroom, there to be reinforced but rarely changed.

Because the media influences the outcomes of trials, should we restrain it in some manner? While we believe democratic ideals in theory, in practice we want watchdogs to protect us individually from governmental excess. Those watchdogs are the press and we are loath to restrain or repress it. The judicial goal of protecting the integrity of its system insures press and public access and outweighs the harm the media can cause in a particular case.

Extensive media coverage caused the 1954 murder conviction of Dr. Sam Sheppard to be reversed. The court determined extensive coverage affected the jury. The Oklahoma City bomber, Timothy McVeigh was the subject of so much international publicity the court decided he couldn't receive a fair trial anywhere in the state. In numerous change of venue cases, judges have concluded jurors would be unable to set aside preconceived notions of guilt. There is no reason not to assume the same is true for innocence, although there is never an appeal of a verdict in favor of an accused defendant found not guilty, therefore appellate courts do not address the issue from that viewpoint. Only the court of public opinion decides if a guilty person was found innocent based on juror preconceptions, and history is often the deciding factor as in the Lizzie Borden and Sacco and Vanzetti cases. O.J. Simpson may well find history does not treat him as well as did the criminal case jury. Arguably the courts failed Sacco and Vanzetti. However, they had the opportunity to have appellate courts review their convictions highlighting the fact those found guilty can appeal. On the other hand, neither the public or their representatives can appeal a finding of innocence because an individual cannot be put in jeopardy more than once; there is no double jeopardy. Our system is balanced in favor of individual defendants and this is intentional. While the United States is a democracy, which simply means the majority rules, the opposite is true when we think of our individual rights. These we jealously protect, often against the majority, because that is the method our forefathers used to satisfy the distrust individuals had and still have for majority rule. The fact is we have a democracy but do not trust it to work for us individually. The old government maxim the "greatest good for the greatest number" is generally rejected because it justifies the compromise of individual rights which is unacceptable to us individually.

Chapter 3

State of Illinois v.
Nathan Leopold Jr. and Richard Loeb

IN THE EARLY MORNING of May 22, 1924, workmen found the naked body of 14 year old Bobby Franks wedged into the mouth of a storm culvert. A few feet away was a single sock and a pair of horne drimmed glasses. The glasses did not belong to Franks. At the time the body was found, the boy's father, Jacob Franks, was at home awaiting a telephone call to tell him where to drop the kidnappers' demand for $10,000 in old bills. Mr. Franks had been advised by telephone that his son had been kidnapped and by a special delivery letter that he was to produce the money. Of course, he was told not to contact the police and he did not do so. It was his intention to cooperate fully with the kidnappers. The amount was small, he was a rich man. He started out in Chicago as a money lender to gamblers and others and had managed to accumulate a fortune in Chicago real estate. His home was diagonally across the street from that of Richard Loeb, in the Hyde Park area of Chicago, a very wealthy neighborhood.

Within a short time, the horn-rimmed glasses were identified as belonging to Richard Loeb, age 18, who frequently bird watched in the area where the body was found. A confession was obtained which implicated his friend Nathan Leopold, age 19, in the murder. At that time the case was considered to be the "crime of the century" because no one could determine the motive of Leopold or Loeb, both highly intelligent sons of wealthy parents. It was proposed that they committed the crime to see if they could get away with it, to display how smart they were. They did it because they could. Obviously, they botched the crime and after their confessions there was no choice but to withdraw their previous plea of not guilty and enter a plea of guilty. Their attorneys' goal was to obtain sentences less than death. Under Illinois law murder was punishable by imprisonment of 14 years to life or death. There was no issue of insanity because the crime was premeditated and the two defendants were highly intelligent. Their attorneys determined that although the crime showed seriously sick minds there was no possibility of proving they could not tell the difference between right and wrong, hence the guilty plea.

The lengthy trial held before Judge John R. Caverly, sitting without a jury, was closely followed because the defense attorneys, particularly Clarence Darrow, argued that based on the defendants' youth the law should recognize degrees of mental responsibility in mitigating sentences. The prosecution contended there was no recognition in the law regarding "degrees of responsibility". They argued either total responsibility for consequences of an act or no responsibility at all. The defense attorneys wanted to show a mental condition that amounted to an illness, and not a physical brain disorder, that could somehow affect the capacity of the defendants to choose between right and wrong. They argued there was sufficient support for this functional mental disease position hence it should be considered in mitigation for sentencing purposes although it was not sufficient to support the complete defense of insanity.

After hearing three days of arguments regarding how to approach the issue, the court (the judge) determined that the law gave it power to hear evidence in mitigation as well as evidence in aggravation for the purposes of sentencing; therefore, the Court decided it would hear the defense evidence and not predetermine the issue. As a result of the Court's decision, it heard testimony from psychiatrists, neuropsychiatrists and other physicians.

In summary, Nathan Leopold, Jr. entered college at age 15, fancied himself as being highly intellectual, had no particular interest in the opposite sex and, after engaging in some small time thefts to prove to himself he was smarter than others and could escape punishment, he plotted the kidnapping of Bobby Franks purely as an intellectual effort. He was straightforward with the doctors and stated he would never commit such a crime again because now he knows it is possible he would be discovered whereas before the crime, he did not think he could be caught.

Richard Loeb entered college at age 14 having completed high school in two years. He also was highly intelligent but with a inferiority complex because he was infirm and impotent. He planned the crime with Leopold because he also thought they could get away with it but he found the actual killing of Bobby Franks with a chisel to be disquieting.

It was the brilliant argument of Clarence Darrow that resulted in the Court not imposing death sentences on the two defendants. Darrow's plea for enlightened compassion because of the youth of the defendants, their emotional makeup, and the irrationality of the crime itself is still considered to be a practical position to take in similar circumstances. Clarence Darrow represented railroads but was also known to defend working-class people and his involvement in this "rich-boy case" in which there was no factual defense nor insanity plea available, was based upon his belief that the execution of teenagers was cruel. In pleading for their lives he asked for understanding, charity, kindness and mercy.

Darrow started his argument by pointing out the crime and trial had generated enormous publicity. He acknowledged the nature of the crime along with the publicity resulted in a demand by the public for the punishment of death. He pointed out that money was not an asset for the defense but, in fact, a burden. He argued the wealth of the defendants further prompted the State attorney to demand the death penalty and the families' prosperity had also generated a public cry for the ultimate punishment.

Darrow advised the Court there had never been anyone in the State of Illinois hung under the age of 23 if they had pled guilty to the crime. He was responding to the State's argument that the law was replete with death sentences being given to children, even those under 14. The State had even quoted from Blackstone, a noted 19th Century British legal scholar:

> "Under 14, though an infant shall be judged to be incapable of guile prima fascia, yet if it appeared to the Court and the jury that he was capable of guile, and could discern between good and evil, he may be convicted and suffer death."

The defense attorney admitted no one wanted the boys to be released, not even their families or friends. Interestingly, he commented that when a jury finds a defendant guilty there is shared responsibility for the death sentence. However, in this case it was the Judge alone who had to deliberately and with premeditation impose that sentence. Darrow noted there previously had been 90 executions in Chicago since 1840 and only four on a plea of guilty. Darrow argued the specifics of two individuals in the history of Cook County who were hung after a plea of guilty and pointed out the last one was sentenced to death by then Judge Crowe who was now the State's attorney in this prosecution. He asked Judge Caverly not to look to the past with hatred and cruelty, but to look to the future and reminded him hanging was not really a punishment, it was an exhibition to others which should be done away with.

At the time of his argument Darrow had practiced law for 45 years and remarked he had never tried a case where the State's attorney did not say it was the most cold-blooded, inexcusable, premeditated case that ever occurred. If it was a robbery, it was the worst; if it was a conspiracy, it was the most terrible and if it were a murder, there never was such a murder. He then pointed out that to make this crime the most cruel thing that ever happened, there would have to be a motive. The State argued the motive was $10,000 because Leopold and Loeb were heavy gamblers and needed the money to pay their debts. Darrow then dismissed the evidence which was simply testimony one of the boys had lost $90.00 in a bridge game at college and explained, at the very time of the crime, Loeb had $3,000 in his own checking account and owned liberty bonds. Leopold regularly received $125.00 a month, had an automobile and paid nothing for board and clothes. He obtained money whenever he wanted it and had arranged a trip to Europe (which was interrupted by his arrest).

Darrow picked away at the State's argument by showing the defendants' motives were not based on the usual notorious reasons for committing murder, i.e., sex, greed, money or relationship. Other than the taking of Franks' life, there was no cruelty, hatred or revenge involved; in fact, there was no really sane reason for committing the crime. Darrow was using the very senselessness of the crime to show that it was an act of diseased brains. He stated:

"Without any excuse, without the slightest motive, not moved by money, not moved by passion or hatred, by nothing except the vague wonderings of children, they rented a machine (car), and about four o'clock in the afternoon started to find somebody to kill. For nothing."

He argued that the very sentence stated in the law, for premeditated murder, hanging, life imprisonment or for a term of 14 years or more, reflects the growing feeling among enlightened people in the United States against capital punishment. "Undoubtedly, through the deep reluctance of courts and juries to take human life." He asked the question: "Do you think you can cure the hatreds and the mal-adjustments of the world by hanging them? You simply show your ignorance and your hate when you say it. You may here and there cure hatred with love and understanding but you can only add fuel to the flames by cruelty and hate." Darrow was rebutting the State's argument which was to "Give them the same mercy they gave to Bobby Franks." After arguing the senseless motivation of the crime, Darrow attacked the "scheming" that led to it. Darrow used the ineptitude and ludicrousness of the plot to emphasize the plan must be a product of diseased minds, a scheme of infancy, of fools and of irresponsibility.

In addition, the defense attorney spent quite a while pointing out to the Court that in most cases there are plea bargains and that the Court normally readily accepts guilty pleas to a lesser offense and takes into consideration the willingness of the defendant to plead guilty when sentencing. Next Darrow spoke of the publicity that would be generated throughout the world if the boys were put to death. He contended there was not a philosopher or religious leader of any creed in the Christian community who would condone hanging the defendants for an immature, childish, purposeless act, conceived without the slightest malice. He also stated he was not so much even pleading for the defendants but for all of those youth to follow who perhaps could not be as well defended as Leopold and Loeb.

Darrow argued at length that all psychiatrists involved in the case stated the boys showed absolutely no emotion regarding the crime. They approached it as a matter of intellect and not emotion. He wondered why these boys, with every opportunity, plenty of wealth and who would have been eminently successful in life would in one day, by an act of madness, destroy all that, so the best they could hope for was a life sentence. "How did it happen?" he asked. He answered the question by giving lengthy explanations of the backgrounds of the two defendants. He took Loeb first, noting he had been under the thumb of a governess from age two through 13. She pushed him to learn and basically he had no fun whatsoever except when he could entertain himself by scheming and sneaking out at night. He found enjoyment in reading stories of crime and mystery. He fancied himself as an amateur detective and thought about committing the perfect crime. Darrow noted that just the year before the State of Illinois passed a statute stating minors were precluded from reading crime stories (the constitutionality of this is left for another discussion) because reading such stories tended to involve youth in crime. The defense attorney presented a supposition that had the Court sent the boy to be analyzed at a state mental hospital, no doubt they would have traced everything back to the gradual growth of the child. Interestingly, today it is quite common for Judges to obtain an assessment of the defendant from many different experts before imposing sentence in numerous types of cases.

Darrow left his argument for "Babe" Leopold for last because he was the older of the two boys. He grew up without a mother and with an absentee father. All the money he needed, as well as cars, were made available to him. He became enamored with the philosophy of

Nietzsche who espoused that from time to time supermen were born, so intelligent they were beyond good and evil. He argued laws for good and evil could not apply to this type of individual. At ages 16, 17 and 18 when other healthy boys were playing baseball or working on farms, Leopold was reading Nietzsche. He became obsessed with some of the doctrines Nietzsche espoused such as supermen have no duty to most others, only to their equals, also individuals of genius are free from such scruples. In summary, Darrow argued:

> "Here is a boy who by day and by night, in season and out, was talking of the superman, owing no obligations to anyone; whatever gave him pleasure he should do, believing it just as another man might believe a religion or any philosophical theory."

He challenged the Court to imagine such thinking coming from anything but a diseased mind.

The State's arguments were put on by a tag team of assistant State's attorneys starting out with Thomas Marshall. He insisted the punishment be proportionate to the offense and that death was the only penalty that applied to a premeditated, carefully planned and deliberate murder of a helpless 14-year-old school boy. He was followed by assistant State's attorney Joseph Savage who went over the facts of the case and was severely chastised by the Judge for referring to an unproven allegation, that Nathan Leopold, Jr. had stated if he could secure a friendly judge, he could beat the case.

The State's arguments were summed up by the State's attorney Robert E. Crowe, a 1901 Yale graduate and Chief Justice of the Cook County Criminal Court in 1920 before being elected State's attorney. Initially, he started out defending Marshall and then Savage, his assistants, who Darrow accused of being heartless and of living up to the latter's name.

Crowe remarked that Clarence Darrow was well-known to be against the death penalty and gave examples of his attempts to affect change at the level of his office as well as the State legislature. He tried to refute Darrow's argument that the death penalty is not a deterrent by focusing on the year 1920 when he was presiding judge of this same court. He brought four additional judges into the court between May 5th and July 1st to try nothing but murder cases. During that brief time of less than 60 days, 15 men were sentenced to death in the Criminal Court of Cook County. He argued the records of the police department, and the records of the Chicago Crime Commission, showed that as a result, murder fell 51% in Cook County during the year 1920. He used that same analogy regarding special prosecution of car thieves and other types of criminals and ended up by stating, "The Rolls Royce became just as safe as the Fivver (an inexpensive automobile) on the streets of Chicago." Although he admitted not having much use for English law (because he was Irish), he stated, "There, justice is handed out swiftly and surely, and as a result there are less murders in the entire Kingdom of Great Britain yearly than there are in the City of Chicago."

Next he argued the power of choice. "These two defendants were perverts, Loeb the victim and Leopold the aggressor, and they quarreled. They entered into a childish pact so that their unnatural crimes might continue." (There were portions of experts' reports that indicated the defendants engaged in sexual acts between themselves but because of their "depravity" that information was excerpted from the reports and not published). He argued the actual motive was the $10,000 ransom that was demanded.

State's Attorney Crowe asked the question, "If these two defendants are suffering from a mental disease, what is the name of it? No one has gone on the stand who has been able to give this mental disease a name. And yet, everyone who testified for the defendants pretended to know all that there was in the books and a great deal that never got into the books." This mental state described by Darrow, was later to become known as diminished capacity.

The State's attorney went through the details of the defendants plotting the crime, and the facts that supported the argument both were involved for financial reasons. The prosecutor advised the Court that while listening to Mr. Darrow plead for sympathy for the two men who showed no sympathy, he was reminded of the story of Abraham Lincoln who represented a young boy who had killed his wealthy parents so that he could inherit their money. When his crime was discovered and the Court asked him the reason why the sentence should not be death, he asked the Court to be lenient because he was a poor orphan.

On September 10, 1924, when Judge Caverly pronounced sentence, he made it clear it was not "mitigating circumstances" that saved the lives of the defendants. He was impressed with Darrow's argument that enlightened humanity was the correct approach.

The defendants were sentenced to life for the murder charge and 99 years for kidnapping. When they realized they were to live, it was reported the frozen expressions on their faces changed and for once they looked like mere boys. The fatalist and mighty Leopold broke down and cried as he was led from the courtroom. Interestingly, the defendants had enough legal knowledge to realize that even if they eventually received a parole on the life sentence they would still have to serve the 99 years for kidnapping and it was this understanding which caused them to lose their composure.

In his summation at the time of sentencing, the Judge found that while careful analysis of the life history of the defendants and their mental, emotional and ethical condition was of extreme interest and potentially valuable to the study of criminology, the Court felt such arguments could be made on behalf of other persons accused of crimes and such analysis would probably reveal similar or different abnormalities.

The Court believed the value of tests was in their applicability to crime and criminals in general. Justice Caverly found the crime was atrocious, repulsive and inhumane. It was deliberately planned and executed with callousness and cruelty. To quash a public perception that had arisen regarding the body being abused after death, the Court specifically stated such did not occur, but the Court also added it did not need that element to make the crime abhorrent. Although Justice Caverly stated he could find no mitigating circumstances, Clarence Darrow's arguments obviously caused the Judge to exercise "enlightened humanity" since he did not render the sentence of death. Darrow's ten hour argument in this case is considered a classic. The United States Supreme Court ruled the execution of minors to be cruel and unusual punishment that is prohibited by the 8th amendment of the United States Constitution. There will be no more executions of those who are minors at the time the crime was committed. Loeb died in prison and Leopold was paroled in the 1950's. He died a few years later.

CHAPTER 4

UNITED STATES V. ROSENBERGS

AS IS CUSTOMARY IN Federal Court, the jury was voir dired by the trial Judge, Irving R. Kaufman; hence it was impaneled in only one and a half days. The Rosenbergs were the subjects of enormous publicity and the case was politically sensitive. Evidence regarding secrets passed to the Russians presented questions of national security. Did the defendants, Ethel and Julius Rosenberg, commit treason by engaging in espionage against the interest of the United States?

Winter was turning to spring in March of 1951. The New York Federal Courthouse in Foley Square, borough of Manhattan was surrounded by those on both sides of the issue. The United States and the United Nations were at war in Korea and the House UnAmerican Activities Committee (HUAC in Washington D.C.) was holding regular hearings. "McCarthyism" was rampant. Individuals were being forced to sign loyalty oaths (University of California), some were being blacklisted (especially in the motion picture industry), and the search for "Reds" was never ending. Since many of Senator McCarthy's hearings were televised, there was much public interest in the case. Defense attorney Emanuel Bloch found himself in the middle of an ethnic and political firestorm.

Although interesting, the facts were fairly simple. During World War II, the "Manhattan Project" was developing the atomic bomb in a number of venues. The center of the effort was located at a newly developed location near Santa Fe, New Mexico called Los Alamos. The actual weapon testing was performed at Trinity Range near Alamogordo, New Mexico approximately 100 miles south of Los Alamos. A scientist named Emil Julius Klaus Fuchs was one of many working at Los Alamos. During the war an enlisted soldier by the name of David Greenglass was also stationed there. Although there were rumors after World War II that some of the United States' atomic secrets had been provided to the Russians, there was no real confirmation of that fact until late 1949 when Klaus Fuchs was interviewed and subsequently arrested in England. The British Secret Service had developed information indicating that the scientist had a Communist Party background. During the investigation, much to their surprise, Fuchs readily acknowledged his wartime espionage activity although it was obvious he did not consider it espionage because at that time the United States was allied with Russia in the war against the axis powers. It was information obtained from Fuchs that led to the subsequent arrest of Harry Gold, David Greenglass and Morton Sobell along with the Rosenbergs. Although Sobell was tried with the Rosenbergs and found guilty, he was not sentenced to death and we will ignore the case against him. Fuchs passed information to Greenglass about a lens device being developed for use in the atomic bomb and Greenglass passed that information on to Harry Gold, Morton Sobell and eventually Julius Rosenberg. Although at the time of the trial there was great controversy concerning the guilt of the Rosenbergs, ensuing events including the collapse of the Soviet empire and a review of Soviet records make it clear he was, in fact, guilty of espionage. The real issue centers around the involvement of Ethel Rosenberg. Independent and historical review of the case indicates that notwithstanding the FBI taking the position that Ethel Rosenberg was the "mastermind" of the espionage ring, it appears she was nothing more than a loyal wife to Julius and a typist who when requested by her husband, typed up information which was passed on. There is no doubt she was guilty of conspiracy to commit espionage; however, had her actual involvement been developed at the time of the trial, it is not likely she would have been given the sentence of death. History asks the questions, was her execution fair and just? Was her sentence supported by the evidence?

During the preparation and prosecution of the case, by Irving Saypol, United States Attorney for the Southern District of New York, assisted by the notorious Roy Cohn who was to become nationally known as counsel for HUAC, the United States government went to great lengths to obtain a confession from Julius Rosenberg in an attempt to have him implicate others. The "lever" or bargaining chip they utilized was keeping pressure on Ethel Rosenberg. It was felt her prosecution and even her subsequent death sentence would cause Julius Rosenberg to confess and involve others. In fact, President Eisenhower made a statement that he thought Ethel Rosenberg was the head of the spy ring. His announcement was based on information provided by the FBI and had no real basis in fact. The President of the United States was actually used to keep the pressure on Julius Rosenberg who could have admitted his involvement and probably saved his wife's life.

Important legal issues in the case were not properly pursued. For example, Klaus Fuchs himself was only imprisoned in England for 14 years because Russia was not an enemy of Great Britain at the time of his actions, hence he could not be found guilty of treason although he was properly found guilty of espionage. This same argument could have been made more forcefully by the attorneys representing the Rosenbergs and, in fact, after their conviction and execution on June

19, 1953, the United States Congress passed a law that became known as the Rosenberg Law. For the first time, the law specifically made any espionage against the interest of the United States in peacetime a capital offense under the treason statute. The traitorous acts no longer had to aid or abet an enemy of the United States.

Ethel Greenglass Rosenberg was born on September 28, 1915 and Julius Rosenberg was born on May 12, 1918. During the early 1930's Julius became a member of the Young Communist League and campaigned for the Scottsboro Boys. He entered City College of New York and became involved in politics. He and Ethel were married in 1939 and in 1942 Julius became a member of the United States Army Signal Corps. In 1943 both Rosenbergs cut off any overt contact with the Communist Party. Thereafter, Julius met with a Soviet spy by the name of Feklisov. In 1944 David Greenglass, Ethel Rosenberg's brother, was stationed at Los Alamos. In late 1944 Rosenberg recruited Greenglass to provide information regarding the Manhattan Project. During late 1944 and early 1945 Greenglass provided notes and sketches. Subsequently Greenglass started meeting with Harry Gold in Albuquerque, New Mexico. This was shortly before the first atomic bomb test at Trinity Range near Alamogordo, New Mexico. Rosenberg and Greenglass left the army and went into business. Their machine shop business failed and David Greenglass blamed Julius Rosenberg for the failure. This provided his motive for later testifying against Rosenberg.

During 1948 Morton Sobell and Max Elitcher, an employee of the Navy ordinance department, met with Rosenberg and provided him microfilmed secret information. Sobell had obtained the information from William Perl who had worked as an engineer at CalTech. He was a leader in the field of aeronautics, specifically jet propulsion mechanisms and design problems related to supersonic flight. This group was considered to be a separate spy ring from the Fuchs Greenglass group although they did connect through Rosenberg.

When the Soviets detonated their first atomic bomb on August 28, 1949, a shockwave went through the United States. Investigations were pursued by both the United States and Great Britain and it was at the end of that year that British intelligence identified Fuchs who was arrested on February 2, 1950. In March 1950, Julius Rosenberg suggested to Greenglass that he leave the country. In May 1950 Rosenberg started making preparations to go to Mexico where Morton Sobell had sought refuge. With the pressure on, Harry Gold confessed to the FBI on May 22, 1950, at which time the Rosenbergs made serious efforts to obtain passports. On June 15, 1950, David Greenglass named Julius as the man who recruited him to spy for the Soviet Union and Rosenberg was immediately interviewed. On July 17, 1950, Julius was arrested at his home and a month later his wife was arrested. In August 1950, Sobell and his family were apprehended by Mexican mercenaries and delivered to the United States authorities at the border. On January 31, 1951, the New York Grand Jury indicted the Rosenbergs, Sobell, David Greenglass and Yakolev who was an associate of the Soviet spy Feklisov. The most shocking evidence in the matter came from David Greenglass and his wife who changed their stories and implicated Ethel Rosenberg, his sister, in the spying activities. David Greenglass was motivated to testify against the Rosenbergs in order to obtain a lighter sentence and because he still harbored a grudge against Julius for allowing their business to fail.

During the trial the government utilized a number of witnesses who made plea bargains and sentencing deals. They were Max Elitcher, Harry Gold, David Greenglass, Ruth Greenglass and Elizabeth Bentley. Basically, the government's case was based upon the evidence of co-conspirators and that is what made the guilty finding questionable in the minds of many.

The United States Supreme Court refused to hear an appeal of the decision by the United States Court of Appeals for the 2nd Circuit in New York upholding the Rosenberg conviction. Shortly before they were to be executed at Sing-Sing Prison on the Hudson River in Ossining, New York, Supreme Court Justice William O. Douglas granted a stay of execution and then left on a trip. This granting of a stay caused wide-spread publicity and cheering among many who believed the Rosenbergs were wrongly convicted but it was short lived since the following day Chief Justice Vinson called a meeting of the court and they vacated Douglas' stay of execution. Apparently, Vinson knew he had the vote to overturn the stay before Douglas left for his trip but for some unknown reason he waited until that justice left Washington before calling a meeting and issuing the order. The Rosenbergs were executed on June 19, 1953.

In the early 1970's Khrushchev stated the Rosenbergs were involved in spying for the Soviet Union. Subsequently declassified cables released by the National Security Agency and Central Intelligence Agency showed the involvement of Julius Rosenberg. Their spymaster Feklisov admitted his meetings with Julius between 1943 and 1946. Finally, in an effort to set the record straight, David Greenglass admitted that he perjured himself in his testimony regarding his sister Ethel Rosenberg's role in the conspiracy.

Although it appears they were both guilty of the charges, Ethel Rosenberg's sentence was arguably not just. Normally, she would have received a sentence of ten to 15 years imprisonment. She was the victim of government manipulation in an effort to have her husband confess and name names and that effort continued right up to their execution.

Justice Blackman of the United States Supreme Court has offered his view that it is delusion to believe our system of justice is fair with regard to how it deals with the penalty of death. In many areas of the United States public perception lends great support to the death penalty. However those that analyze how it is administered often accept the opinion of Justice Blackman.

Putting moral issues aside, because they are more emotional and subjective, when one studies the facts, it is difficult to conclude our system is fair and therefore just. Should one arrive at that point, the moral issues become much clearer.

Retribution is not a morally reprehensible goal and if society decides, as it has in many jurisdictions, that the goal is worthy, it is hard to controvert an eye for an eye approach. However, it is less difficult to disagree if the goal is pursued in an unfair and unjust manner. Most individuals do not believe the end justifies the means, and if in fact the means are not generally considered fair, support for the death penalty would erode. If a system is developed that is objectively fair, a society can justify its use of the death penalty to obtain retribution as well as satisfy the good of being a deterrent.

Therefore, the real question is does our system of justice use fair means to arrive at a final decision and resulting execution. One can certainly argue Sacco-Vanzetti were the victims of an unfair process. Has the system improved? Many would argue it has not. Trumped up evidence is very unlikely in modern trials. However, poor lawyering as well as the inability of the defendant to understand the charges, the evidence and the workings of the system still exists in many cases. This recognition finally resulted in the U.S. Supreme Court finding that the death penalty, as it applies to minors whose decision making abilities are not fully developed, is a cruel and unusual punishment pursuant to the 8 th Amendment of the United States Constitution; hence, it is prohibited. Clarence Darrow's arguments in Leopold and Loeb finally became the law of the land some 70 years later proving that old trials often are instructive in dealing with present day issues.

Changing standards of decency are now important to the U.S. Supreme Court which accepts the moral view that an unjust method of punishment exists in death cases under certain circumstances. Scientific advancements now allow the testing of physical evidence (as in the case of DNA) resulting in the release of numerous convicted individuals from the death rows of prisons in many states. Our system has put numerous individuals in death row, oftentimes unjustly, for many years. We should recognize our methods are not always fair, hence they are arguably unjust.

It is obvious to many who have studied individual cases that defendants with wealth, who can retain excellent counsel, rarely receive the death penalty. Those who do receive it are generally on the margins or below the median measure of society in intelligence, economics, and the support of family, friends and meaningful segments of our society. Often the death penalty is decided based upon a few points of IQ. For instance, in many jurisdictions if an IQ is 70 or less, the defendant is considered retarded and cannot be executed while a person with an IQ a few points higher can receive the death penalty and be executed. Is the difference in score arbitrary, hence the death penalty unjust?

Some argue that justice delayed is not justice at all, either for the family and friends of the victim or the defendant. Cases that are on appeal for ten to 15 years or occasional 20 to 25 years cause the credibility of our justice system to be strained. It fails to bring closure in a timely manner and often exacerbates the pain and grief of those involved because they cannot put it behind them.

Most countries of the world recognize their inability to sustain a fair system of imposing the death penalty and no longer use it. The

United States along with a few other countries such as China, Pakistan, Iran, and Somalia retain it. Should our system be determined unfair, it cannot be morally justified. On the other hand, if a system is fair and just in its means and methods, meaning the death penalty is consistently applied using objective criteria in a timely manner and the accused has had the benefit of competent counsel throughout the proceedings, the moral issue should be less of an imperative and society, by majority rule, should be able to exact retribution if it determines such is an appropriate goal. All to often this is not the situation and not much is being done to improve the system. In all likelihood, little will be done as long as the public supports the system which exists.

A total analysis of the fairness issue would take volumes and unfortunately the issue is often overshadowed by bias in the first instance. It is certainly beyond the goal of this work. Once a person seeks objective information, their opinions and views of the death penalty issue can change. Even a lifelong death penalty supporter can have a change of view after studying the issue.

Ronald George, former Chief Justice of the California Supreme Court, stated, recently stated, "We are concerned with speed and efficiency, but we are also concerned about fairness." The Federal Government passed "fast track" legislation ten years ago, however, the states have not implemented the necessary procedures. After 24 years on death row, California executed Stanley "Tookie" Williams, the founder of the Los Angeles Crips gang. Speed and efficiency equaling fairness should not take 24 years.

CHAPTER 5

TENNESSEE V. SCOPES

THE JURY WAS COMPRISED of male residents of Rhea County and included farmers, a teacher (who read the Bible on a regular basis), a merchant, a United States marshal, a shipping clerk, a cabinet maker, and a carpenter. It is worth noting nearly all jurors were practicing Baptists or Methodists. Presided over by County Judge John T. Ralston, the trial began on July 10, 1925, the place Dayton, Tennessee.

The jury was selected on a Friday afternoon and the following Monday court opened with a prayer by the Rev. Moffett referring to God as Our Creator, Preserver and Controller of All Things. He asked for blessings upon the Court, the jury, the lawyers, the newspapermen, and the ideals of justice.

Attorney General Stewart, prosecuting, asked the Court to again voir dire a juror named Gentry because it was reported he had expressed the opinion Scopes was innocent. Defense attorney Clarence Darrow objected because the jury panel had already been selected, but since it had not yet been sworn, the Court allowed further interrogation. Mr. Gentry convinced the Court he had an open mind and he remained on the jury. The jury was sworn and the indictment read. Scopes was accused of teaching a theory of evolution that denies the story of the

Divine Creation, as taught in the Bible, and instead taught that man evolved from a lower order of animals, all against the peace and dignity of the state. It was alleged he did so as a teacher in the public schools of Rhea County,.

The specific legal issue was the State of Tennessee's charge that John T. Scopes violated Chapter 27 of the Acts of 1925, generally known as the Anti-Evolution Statute, which made it unlawful to teach in the public schools of the State of Tennessee any theory contrary to the Biblical account of Divine Creation. Shortly after it was passed, John T. Scopes, a teacher, was indicted for violation of the statute, which carried the penalty of a $100 to $500 fine. The Grand Jury that indicted Scopes was told by the Court that the description of Creation which applied was set forth in the first chapter of Genesis. The jury had to determine his guilt or innocence.

The defense moved the Court to quash the indictment on the basis the statute was in violation of the Constitution of Tennessee. Numerous provisions of the Constitution were referred to, most were general in nature. However, it did provide "that no human authority can, in any case whatsoever, control or interfere with the rights of conscious; and that no preference shall ever be given, by law, to any religious establishment or mode of worship."

The Tennessee Constitution also provided for freedom of speech as well as freedom of thought and opinion. The document specifically referred to the Fourteenth Amendment of the United States Constitution which states, "No state shall make or enforce any law which shall abridge the privileges or immunities of citizens of the United States. Nor shall any state deprive any person of life, liberty, or property without due process of law, nor to deny to any person within the jurisdiction the equal protection of the laws." After making the motion, the defense asked the Court to take it under submission and not rule until after the

Court heard the evidence produced during the trial. In presenting the motion the defense pointed out that trial courts possess the same power as appellate courts to decide a law unconstitutional and that the defense would eventually ask the Court to exercise that power. Interestingly, during these arguments the jury, which had been empanelled but had not yet received any evidence, was present in the courtroom. General Stewart objected to their presence. In response, the defense argued the jury should be able to hear its position. The Court responded that whether or not the jury was present was a matter of its discretion; therefore, it exercised discretion and excused the jury. While the Court's ruling was correct, it was too late. How do you unring a bell? The jury had already heard the legal arguments presented regarding the unconstitutionality of the charge.

The prosecution argued the charge was based upon a proper exercise of police power to preserve public safety and public morals and that it was not an undue restriction upon individual liberties. The defense argued the law made expressions illegal in a public school room when they would not be illegal on the streets of the towns, in private homes or in any other location. The issues of appropriate police power were argued along with the State's interest in the subject matter of the statute. The Court declared these constitutional issues were profound and could not be decided on an empty stomach—hence, the Court adjourned for lunch.

After lunch, in a very warm Courtroom, the Court allowed counsel to remove their coats. General Stewart responded to the defense motions. He argued the State legislature was confronted by a conflict between literature and science. He stated the law expressed the policy or the belief of people at the time. There was discussion of precedence dealing with public policy issues and it was shown that the legislature has discretion to set policy. The defense countered that the Attorney General had admitted there was no science to support the Biblical explanation of Creation. The prosecution took the position that the law did not interfere with religious worship, it only addressed itself directly to the public school system of the State. Darrow argued the constitutional provision "no preference shall ever be given, by law, to any religious establishment or mode of worship," and that the statute gave such a preference to the Bible. The prosecution responded there was nothing in the statute that gave preference to any religious establishment or mode or worship. Questions arose regarding what version of the Bible pertained. The Attorney General claimed in that area of the country, the King James version was most accepted. At one point General Stewart was forced to state, "The legislature, according to our laws, in my opinion, would have the right to preclude the teaching of geography. He responded when asked, "Does the law prefer the Bible to the Koran?" The statute does not mention the Koran. When pressed Stewart stated, "We are not living in a heathen country."

When discussing the United States Constitution's 14th Amendment, the prosecution argued it dealt with property rights and that the statute did not take away Mr. Scopes' property rights because no one has a vested right, a civil right or an inherent right to be a teacher in a public school. They argued the law was sufficient to notify the defendant what he is charged with and that the indictment was sufficiently specific to proscribe the conduct it prohibited. The prosecution stated it was not vague, and that a 16 year old could understand it. The prosecution concluded the statute was not void for indefiniteness or uncertainty. The case of Meyer v. Nebraska was cited. In that matter Nebraska prohibited the teaching in any schools in the state (not just the public schools, but all schools) any language other than English to any pupil under the eighth grade. The United States Supreme Court held that the statute invaded the right of property inasmuch as it precluded the instructor from teaching German in private and parochial schools, thereby depriving him of his right to pursue a lawful occupation. However, the Court in that case stated the law was unconstitutional because it affected all schools, not just public schools. The Court stated, "The power of the State to compel attendance at some schools and to make reasonable regulations for all schools including a requirement they shall give instruction in English is not questioned. Nor has challenge been made of the State's power to prescribe curriculum for institutions which it supports. Those matters are not within the present (Meyer) controversy." General Stewart argued <u>Meyer v. Nebraska</u> authorized the legislature to prescribe conduct in public schools. "How much stronger could they make the language? How much more, Your Honor, would we have them say to recognize the right of the State of Tennessee to direct and control the curriculum in the Rhea County High School? That is the question, I think that it is settled; that is the highest tribunal of our nation speaking."

A discussion ensued regarding whether or not the State controlled the textbook which Mr. Scopes used while teaching. The prosecution admitted there was no law regarding that point but that the State would have a right to do so. The defense asked, "How did he get the book? We mean, was it given to him by the State," and the prosecution replied, "That is a matter of proof; we are prepared to show that; do you want to put me on the witness stand?"

During the early stages of the trial reference was made on a number of occasions to the defense attorneys being from up north and the Judge referred to them as foreigners. On the other hand, the Judge bestowed the title of "colonel" on Clarence Darrow who stated, "I shall always remember that this Court is the first one that ever gave me a great title of 'colonel' and I hope it will stick to me when I get back north." The Court responded, "I want you to take it back to your home with you,

Colonel." Actually the defense included attorneys from California, Chicago, Florida and New York. Darrow argued this trial could be likened to a struggle between two civilizations.

Colonel Darrow quoted Bancroft, a noted legal scholar, "That it is all right to preserve freedom in constitutions, but when the spirit of freedom has fled, from the hearts of the people, then its matter is easily sacrificed under law." He went on to say, "And so it is, unless there is left enough of the spirit of freedom in the State of Tennessee, and in the United States, there is not a single line of any constitution that could withstand bigotry and ignorance when it seeks to destroy the rights of the individual; and bigotry and ignorance are ever active. Here, we find today as brazen and as bold an attempt to destroy learning as was ever made in the Middle Ages, and the only difference is we have not provided that they shall be burned at the stake, but there is time for that, Your Honor, we have to approach these things gradually." He goes on to state, "All the guarantees go for nothing. All of the past is gone, will be forgotten, if this can succeed." He was a powerful force in the courtroom.

Darrow emphasized numerous points, the most important being:

1. The caption of the act stated it was to prohibit the teaching of the evolution theory in Tennessee, yet there is not one word about evolution in the act.
2. Tennessee law requires the caption must state the substance and meaning of the act and the act can contain nothing excepting the substance of the caption.
3. He argued no legislature can say what is divine and that the Bible is a book primarily of religion and morals and not of science. He explained it is 66 books, written over a period of about 1,000 years. It is not a work on astronomy, biology or

evolution. He argued evolution is still a mystery. Although an admitted agnostic, Darrow noted he found no fault with religion. He argued there were two conflicting accounts in the first two chapters of the Bible. The uncertainty and impossibility of recognizing whether one is teaching something contrary to the Bible so as to commit a crime made the act unconstitutional. Specifying there were over 500 different sects or churches in the United States, he stressed a school teacher must not only know the subject he is teaching, but he must know everything about the Bible in reference to evolution, otherwise he might violate the statute and that no criminal statute can be that indefinite. It is basic in criminal law that a statute must specifically describe the prohibited conduct to be valid. Darrow stated, "If Mr. Scopes is to be indicted and prosecuted because he taught a wrong theory of the origin of life, why not tell him what he must teach. Why not say that you must teach that man was made of the dust; and still, strange or not, directly from the dust, without taking any chances on it, and whatever, that Eve was made out of Adam's rib."

Judge Raulston had a different clergyman every day open the proceedings with prayer. This was objected to by defense counsel after the first day as being inappropriate especially in the case in question. They argued the local community, newspapers, etc. were adverse to the defense position and to have the Court, not only sanction, but actively participate in prayer was prejudicial to the defendant. The Court overruled their objections. Interestingly, after the Court ruled on the prayer issue, it received a petition from the "Pastors Association" of the town requesting the Court allow other ministers to open the daily session with prayer who were not from fundamentalists religions. They stated there are many to whom the prayers of the fundamentalists are not spiritually uplifting and are occasionally offensive. Inasmuch as by your own ruling all the people in the courtroom are required to participate in the prayers by rising, it seems to us only just and right that we should occasionally hear a prayer which requires no mental reservations on our part and with which we can conscientiously participate." The Court ruled henceforth the Pastors Association would choose the minister to give the opening prayer each day.

The Judge also had to deal with newspaper publications throughout the country that purported to report the decision he made on motions he took under submission. He had a meeting at the end of the third day of trial with representatives of the press and appointed a number of them to a committee to ascertain the facts of the newspaper reports. Obviously, the Court was annoyed the papers were stating he had already decided to find the statute constitutional and overrule the objections of the defense. At the end of his meeting with the press the Judge stated he would announce his decision the following day. He also discovered his own action caused a newspaperman to prematurely print his decision to overrule the motion to quash the indictment. Apparently, a reporter asked the Judge at midday on the third day of trial if he would rule that afternoon and the Court stated it was its intention to do so. The reporter then asked if the Court would adjourn until the following day and the Judge replied in the affirmative. The reporter concluded as a matter of logic that if the trial was to resume the following day, the Judge intended to deny the motion to quash since if he granted that motion there would be no further trial.

Witnesses were called on the fourth through the eighth days of trial, the Bible was entered as an exhibit, much being made of the fact there were different versions such as the Douay Version followed by Catholics and the King James Version claimed by most protestant churches. After the Bible was admitted in evidence through the testimony of a witness named White, a 14-year-old boy named Howard Morgan was called. As a student of "Professor" Scopes, it was established the teacher taught a different theory of creation than that set forth in the Bible and that it was done at the Rhea County High School. He testified they were studying from a general science book that taught man evolved from a little germ spouting in the sea which came onto dry land and became mammals with various classifications; one of which was primates. Next a church-going, 17 year old boy was called. His name was Harry Shelton and as a witness for the prosecution he testified that in his biology class Professor Scopes taught a theory of creation other than what is set forth in the Bible. He also testified Scopes commented that any teacher in the State who was teaching Scopes' textbook, Hunters Biology, was violating the law and that science teachers could not teach Hunters Biology without violating the law.

On the fifth day of trial much time was spent arguing over the admission of expert testimony. The prosecution claimed experts engaged largely in the field of speculation and there was always danger the jury may substitute an expert's opinion for their own. In fact, courts generally do not allow expert testimony when the subject is one jurors would be competent to evaluate without the help of experts. The Court and Clarence Darrow debated whether life came from a single cell and, if so, where the cell came from. General Stewart was willing to accept he probably evolved from a caveman but he would not agree his cells could be traced back to a monkey or an ass. Simply put, the prosecution wanted to bar the door to scientific evidence and stay on the religious side on the basis that expert evidence was wholly irrelevant, incompetent and impertinent to the issues before the Court. The prosecution took the position that since it was not really contested the defendant did the acts alleged, there was no need for expert testimony on which the defense case was largely based. The Court ruled in favor of the prosecution but in deference to the defense stated it would allow their experts to testify outside the presence of the jury so that the court record would reveal to an appellate court the position of the defendant.

The prosecution asked the Court for the right to cross-examine experts but Darrow objected stating they did not actually intend to call witnesses. They simply wanted to present to the Court, a written summary of the essence of their defense. In the court record it is obvious Darrow became somewhat short with Judge Raulston because the Court took too long to decide motions and he believed the Court was one-sided. These exchanges occurred on a Friday afternoon and Judge Raulston waited until Monday morning before he cited Darrow for contempt, ordered him to appear in court on July 21, 1925 and required he post a $5,000 bond to insure his appearance. On the seventh day of the trial the Judge forgave "Colonel" Darrow and the attorney apologized.

During the sixth and seventh days of the trial numerous declarations of scientists were entered into the record, other bibles were introduced and finally the defense surprised everyone by calling as a witness special counsel to the prosecution, Williams Jennings Bryan. Since the witness did not object to being called, the Judge allowed it, provided he was asked no questions requiring him to answer confidential attorney-client matters. Darrow established Bryan had studied the Bible in depth. It was also established he published articles and other writings regarding interpretations of the Bible. The witness pointed out he had studied the Bible for 50 years and testified he believed everything should be accepted, although some passages were illustrative and not literally true. He was questioned regarding the veracity of the stories of Jonah and the whale and Joshua making the sun stand still. Darrow started cross-examining Bryan and the prosecution objected because one cannot cross-examine their own witness. However, Darrow explained to the

Court the witness had become hostile and that is an exception to the rule. Darrow was allowed to proceed.

Bryan charged the defense with evil motives. He stated, "These gentlemen have not had much chance. They did not come here to try this case. They came here to try revealed religion. I am here to defend it, and they can ask me any question they please. Because of this statement, the Court allowed Darrow to continue, but it soon turned ugly with the lawyer and the witness exchanging insults. Darrow went on to question the witness regarding the Great Flood, when it occurred and whether all living things not contained in the ark were destroyed. Bryan thought they were destroyed except perhaps for fish. Bryan asserted he did not believe, based on evidence he had, that there were any civilizations on this earth reaching back beyond 5,000 years. Darrow was relentless in his questioning Bryan's assertions about the flood being in 2300 B.C and the beginning of civilization. Bryan would not acknowledge there were civilizations such as China that are six or seven thousand years old. He did not accept any civilization would "run back beyond the Creation, according to the Bible 6,000." The cross-examination went on to compare Christianity, Confucianism and Buddhism.

When trial started on the eighth day the Judge stated he was probably in error allowing Mr. Bryan to testify. Therefore he ordered the testimony stricken from the record. At this time the defense rested since it had no witnesses to actually controvert the specific charge against Scopes. Darrow advised the Court that although they continued to claim the defendant was not guilty, because the Court had excluded any testimony except as to whether his teachings reflected that man evolved from a lower order of animals, and since the defense could not contradict that testimony, there was no logical result other than a verdict from the jury of guilty which they intended to carry to a higher court.

Thereafter the Judge charged the jury giving the usual general instructions regarding what the State had to prove for them to find the defendant guilty. He gave the "beyond a reasonable doubt" instruction which does not include any possible doubt that might arise, or such doubt as an ingenuous mind might conjure up, but reasonable in the mind of a reasonable person. It does not mean absolutely no doubt; it does mean there should not be much doubt or such doubt as would prevent a mind resting easy as to the guilt of the defendant. He charged the jury regarding how they must weigh evidence including the credibility of witnesses.

Darrow advised the jury, in essence, that under the evidence they did not have much choice but to find Scopes guilty, since he had not put on a defense. He explained they had come to produce evidence, but the Court had not allowed it and that the final determination in this case would be made by a higher court. The Attorney General chose not to address the jury. It was obvious to everyone there was but only one result which could occur.

There was discussion between counsel and the Court regarding the amount of a fine and, as we should all remember, prohibition was in effect at that time. The least fine in a whiskey transportation case was $100 and that the Court believed this was no more serious. The Court did give the jury the option to fix the fine between $100 or $500. The jury found Scopes guilty and declined to impose a fine thereby leaving it to the Court. The Court did, in fact, fine him $100. Upon conviction Scopes advised the Court he felt he had been convicted of violating an unjust statute and that he would continue in the future, as he had in the past, to oppose the law in any way he could. He stated any other action would be in violation of his ideals of academic freedom — that is, to teach the truth as guaranteed in our constitution, of personal and religious freedom.

Defense counsel made a motion for a new trial which was denied by the Court. After thanking the people of the area for their hospitality, Darrow compared the trial to that of the witchcraft trials and remarked that great events occur in small places such as Dayton. He compared the town to a smaller place where the Magna Charta was wrested from the barons in England. The last statement in the case was made by defense lawyer, Hays, who stated he would send the Judge a copy of Charles Darwin's Origin of Species and the Descent of Man. The Judge stated, "Yes — yes." The courtroom erupted in laughter and applause. But before anyone could leave, the Court asked Dr. Jones to say a benediction. Only then did the Court adjourn the proceeding.

The issue was also adjourned only to resurface 70 years later. In 2004, another court heard similar arguments in a Pennsylvania case. Now God is called by some an intelligent designer, by others, a higher power. Pennsylvania plaintiffs sued in Federal Court in opposition to the Dover School District Board's order to teach 9th grade biology students that the theory of evolution was not totally proven because the world is so complex, it must have been created by some intelligent being with powers higher than human beings. In 2006 a Federal Judge determined the theory of intelligent design is synonymous with religious creationism.

Previously, creationists and evolutionists opposed each other in the United States Supreme Court in 1987, and the Court held creationism could not be taught in schools because the First Amendment required government be separate from religion. Now some scientists, generally religious conservatives, do in fact side with creationists. Others oppose state university websites which refer to some religions not being against the theory of evolution which is the equivalent of a government entity commenting on religion. Further evidence of the contemporary occurrence of the topic is reports of surveys indicating a large percentage of teachers feel pressured to teach creationism. Phillip Johnson, a U.C. Berkeley law professor, reignited this issue by arguing the theory of evolution is a theory, not a fact, and should be taught as such. The battle continues in many states. What Clarence Darrow and William Jennings Bryan argued in 1925 is still a hot issue fueled again in many areas of the United States by a return to religious fundamentalism.

CHAPTER 6

The Scottsboro Boys Trials

On March 24, 1931, Victoria Price age 21, and Ruby Bates age 17, two young, white women, embarked upon a freight train leaving Huntsville, Alabama destined for Chattanooga, Tennessee. That trip was uneventful and they stayed overnight in Chattanooga. On March 25 they boarded another freight train destined for Memphis, Tennessee. While traveling back through Alabama, they claimed four young black men raped Victoria while three others raped Ruby. This supposedly occurred after a confrontation between the black youths and a number of white boys whom the blacks allegedly threw off the train. The exception was a white youth named Orville Gilley, who became a key witness at the subsequent trials. When the white boys exited the train they reported the incident to the station master at Stevenson who telegraphed ahead to Scottsboro 18 miles further west. However the freight train had passed through Scottsboro so that station master telegraphed on to Paint Rock, 20 miles farther and at that location the nine defendants were arrested by a posse. Victoria Price had been adamant there were 12 blacks in the gang and assuming that was the case, three had exited the train before Paint Rock and were never seen or heard from again.

As reflected by the date of the first trial, April 6, 1931, justice was swift. In only two days an all white male jury presided over by Judge Alfred E. Hawkins sitting in the Scottsboro Alabama Circuit Court found all guilty and, except for Roy Wright, all were sentenced to death. One juror held out for life imprisonment for Roy Wright and a mistrial in this case was declared. Between the time of the arrests and this first trial, thousands of people descended on Scottsboro since the matter received wide publicity and most assumed that black men (or in this case, black boys) accused of assaulting and raping two white women would be found guilty and executed. The swiftness of the first trial and verdict seemed to support this view. Because of threats of lynching, the National Guard was called out to keep the defendants in custody and protect the courthouse. The mood locally was "hang 'em" or "fry 'em" but large organizations such as the NAACP and the International Labor Defense Organization (ILD), a communist supported group) came to the defendants' defense. The first trial resulted in the convictions and death sentences of Olen Montgomery, Clarence Norris, Haywood Patterson, Ozzy Powell, Willy Roberson, Charlie Weems, Eugene Williams and Andy Wright. They were immediately ordered executed, however, the judgment was stayed by an appeal to the Alabama Supreme Court. Subsequently, Ruby Bates, in writing, recanted her testimony and stated she had not been raped. Notwithstanding that action, the Alabama Supreme Court affirmed the death sentence of seven and reversed that of Eugene Williams, who was only 14 at the time, therefore a minor and, pursuant to state law, could not be executed. In November 1932, the United States Supreme Court by a vote of 7 to 2 reversed the convictions of all the defendants in the case known as Powell v. State of Alabama on the basis the defendants were not provided adequate assistance of counsel as required by the due process clause of the 14th Amendment. The bottom line is the Court found the defense lawyers incompetent. Thereafter, in January 1933 a respected New York lawyer, Samuel S. Liebowitz, was retained by the ILD to defend the Scottsboro Boys.

Haywood Patterson was tried a second time, in Decatur, before Judge James Edwin Horton, Sr. The trial took place during late March and early April 1933. Again found guilty he was sentenced to death in the electric chair, however, on June 22, 1933, Judge Horton set aside Haywood Patterson's conviction and granted a new trial. The Judge felt the evidence did not support the verdict. He continued the trials of the other Scottsboro Boys because of local tension. The case caused huge protest rallies in Washington and other locations. The judge did not feel the other defendants could get a fair trial. In October 1933 the cases were removed from Judge Horton's jurisdiction and transferred to Judge William Callahan.

Prosecutor Wade Wright again prepared his case. At the November 1935 through January 1936 re-trial of Haywood Patterson, wherein he was joined by defendant Clarence Norris, the two were again convicted of rape and sentenced to death. Again, an appeal to the Alabama Supreme Court resulted in the verdict standing. Further appeal to the U.S. Supreme Court resulted in the convictions being overturned because of obvious jury roll tampering resulting in blacks being systematically excluded from sitting as jurors.

In January 1936, Haywood Patterson was again convicted (for the fourth time) but on this occasion he was not sentenced to death. Instead he was sentenced to 75 years. His conviction was upheld by the Alabama Supreme Court and because the U.S. Supreme Court refused to grant a hearing he served his sentence until he escaped from prison in July 1948. In December 1950 he was involved in an altercation resulting in the death of another and he was charged with murder. In September

1951, he was convicted of manslaughter and sentenced to 6 to 15 years. He died of cancer a year later.

The rest of the Scottsboro boys were convicted and sentenced to various prison terms. All were paroled during the 1940's. Clarence Norris was pardoned by Alabama Governor George Wallace in October 1976. As the last surviving Scottsboro Boy he lived until January 1989.

Obviously, Judge Horton setting aside the second conviction of Haywood Patterson because of insufficiency of the evidence, a rare and noble act, is significant in that at least in the Judge's mind (often judges are considered the 13 th juror), there was reasonable doubt. In fact, the finding of insufficient evidence is much stronger than reasonable doubt especially in the context of this case. Judge Horton was not re-elected and he must have known at the time his action would most likely result in his losing his seat on the bench. The real question is, was any crime committed at all? The evidence, when considered by reasonable minds, was replete with inconsistencies and much of it was incredible. For instance, upon physical examination shortly after the event, the two women showed virtually no evidence of physical abuse and although sperm was present it was "dead" indicating sexual intercourse had occurred some time before the alleged rapes. The backgrounds of the key prosecution witnesses, Victoria Price and Ruby Bates, were ignored by the first defense counsel. Subsequent investigation revealed Victoria Price was a prostitute and given to grandiose statements. Because of Victoria's willingness to take center stage, Bates became upset and some argue that is why she recanted her testimony. A fair review of newspaper publicity at the time leads one to conclude it was virtually impossible for the Scottsboro Boys to receive an impartial trial. They had been convicted and sentenced to death in the newspapers even before the trial. The girls' hometown newspaper, The Huntsville Daily Times, described the rape as "the most atrocious ever recorded in this part of the country, a wholesale debauching of society..." It further stated, "the white men of the South, will not stand for such acts..." It additionally reported, "the nine brutes" had to answer for the "heinous and unspeakable crime."

Initially, the defendants were represented by Steven R. Roddy, a Chattanooga attorney who "seemed adequate enough when sober" according to the chairman of the Chattanooga Commission on Interracial Cooperation. On Monday morning, March 30, 1931 Roddy drove to Scottsboro for a hearing by the Jackson County Grand Jury. The courtroom and courthouse were guarded by three National Guard officers and 30 troops. The senior officer, Major Joe Starnes, allowed spectators but they had to "check their weapons" outside. Only Victoria Price and Orville Gilley testified at the Grand Jury and they immediately indicted the nine at which time Judge Hawkins set trial for the following Monday, April 6. By 7:00 a.m. on that date there were several thousand people clamoring for admission through the National Guard lines and the roofs of all surrounding buildings were packed with spectators. The scene included four machine guns guarding the courthouse doors which gave the appearance the building was a fort under siege. When Roddy appeared the spectators were particularly unfriendly and many cursed him. One of the prosecutors noted the defense lawyer had literally fortified himself with strong spirits against such a contingency. One reported that he was so "stewed" he could "scarcely walk straight". As it developed, appointed counsel Ernest Parks, who really wanted out of the case, suggested Roddy, since he was present, could represent the boys. Roddy pointed out that if he were paid he might be willing to do so but he had not prepared the case for trial and he was unfamiliar with Alabama law since he was a Tennessee lawyer. The trial seemed stalled until Milo Moody stepped forward and stated he would be willing to help Mr. Roddy. This was satisfactory to

Judge Hawkins who told the rest of the Jackson County Bar they no longer had to appear on behalf of the defendants and thus, with no preparation and less than a half hour interview with their lawyers, the nine negro youths went on trial for their lives.

Roddy did have sense enough to ask for a change of venue which was denied. The main witness, Victoria Price, alleged that it took two of them to take her clothes off while four ravished her and "they wouldn't have if they hadn't had knives and guns." She gave an explicit description and pointed out the six, Charlie Weems, Clarence Norris, Roy and Andy Wright, Haywood Patterson, and Olin Montgomery. She was not quite sure about Patterson but at one point adamantly stated, "I know his old mug." She told a story of having been "beaten up" and "bruised up" by the repeated rapes but never stopped fighting. The defense lawyer's strategy was to show she had less than an exemplary character having been married twice, however Judge Hawkins precluded the defense from raising issues about her background.

The next witness, Dr. R.R. Bridges, one of two doctors who examined the girls within an hour and 30 minutes after the alleged rape, stated he found semen in the vaginas of both Victoria Price and Ruby Bates (and in the case of the latter he alleged it was "a great amount"). He also testified Victoria had small bruises about the top of her hips and a few short scratches on the left arm but he emphasized these were minor. When he examined her genital organs he found neither bruises nor tears. "She was not lacerated at all. She was not bloody, and neither was the other girl." He added that the semen found was "non-motile" (dead) and finally he told the jury Victoria Price was not hysterical at all during the time of the examination. He did agree with the prosecution that it was "possible" that four men, one right after the other could have had intercourse with her without lacerations. The second medical witness, Dr. Marvin Lynch, stated he found a large amount of semen in the vagina of Ruby Bates but a very small amount, just enough to make a smear, was obtained from Victoria Price. He also stated that there was nothing to indicate any violence about the vagina.

Ruby Bates testified and her account varied greatly from that of Victoria. Defense counsel did a poor job of cross-examining her. While Victoria talked about guns and knives, Ruby stated that when the black boys entered the railroad car, four of the white boys simply jumped off and the other three put up a small struggle. It was pointed out that when the girls first came into the hands of the posse at Paint Rock, they related the story of the altercation between the white and black boys and mentioned nothing of being raped. The prosecution called a few other witnesses. James Broadway testified he was passing through Paint Rock and was there when Victoria Price "came to the police station" and "I did not hear Victoria Price make any complaint, either to me, or anybody else there, about the treatment she had received at the hands of these defendants over there." This witness did not testify in subsequent trials.

Defendant Weems testified and admitted there had been a fight. He stated Haywood Patterson came along with a pistol in his hand and urged him to help throw several white boys off the train. Patterson told him that some of the boys had tried to knock him off the tanker car where he had been sitting. According to Weems it was not much of a fight. Haywood hit one of the boys and without argument they began jumping off the train. By the time Orville Gilley was ready to jump, the train had reached 40 miles per hour and they helped pull him back into the car. On cross-examination Weems denied the girls were in the car, stating there were just "negroes and one white boy". He did testify several of the "negroes on the train jumped off and he did not see them again." He denied ever seeing a rape or doing anything to the girls. Not having any witnesses for the defense, Roddy and Moody decided to put

Clarence Norris on the stand and he supported Weems' story. On cross-examination Norris, in an attempt to save himself, became unglued and stated "every one of them have something to do with those girls after they put the white boys off the train." Norris described the scene with Roy Wright holding a knife and said that all of the other seven took turns raping the girls except him. The defense lawyers were obviously in shock as their witness shattered their flimsy defense. If Norris had hoped to save himself he got little cooperation from the prosecution. To the defense lawyers the case seemed hopeless and they told the judge they did not care to argue it before the jury. Thereupon the prosecution requested the death penalty and received it quite readily.

The case became the cause celeb of the 1930's. The communist press called it a "legal lynching" resulting from the capitalist bosses of the south and their cohorts throughout the United States violating the rights of the negroes. They were called the "victims of capitalist justice". But it was not only the communists that came to the defense of The Scottsboro Boys. There had been many cases similar to the Scottsboro trial in the south but most had gone unnoticed. Some reports stated there were 5,000 illegal lynchings of black men in the south between 1890 and 1940. Because of the number of participants, their youth, and the harsh sentences a wave of protest was generated across America. The name "Scottsboro" became synonymous with southern racism, repression and injustice. This case was the trigger of the subsequent civil rights movement in the United States which was interrupted by World War II and only waited for a leader thereafter.

These trials highlight the danger of the death penalty. These defendants obtained competent counsel only because of the number of defendants involved and the publicity that garnered. Samual S. Liebowitz became one of the most celebrated trial lawyers of his time.

He consistently prevailed over Tom Dewey, when he was the Manhattan District Attorney. When Dewey became Governor of New York, he appointed Liebowitz to the bench so as to avoid other prosecutors having to deal with him. Unfortunately, many defendants charged with capital crimes in the United States do not have the most competent counsel and their death sentences are, in fact, carried out.

CHAPTER 7

WALKER v. BIRMINGHAM (THE REAL PARTIES IN INTEREST WERE MARTIN LUTHER KING, JR., WYATT WALKER, RALPH ABERNATHY AND A.D. KING)

THE TRIAL IN BIRMINGHAM, Alabama, subsequent state appeal and decision by the United States Supreme Court provides an overview of the civil rights movement as well as showing the different consequences of violation of an unconstitutional law and violation of an unconstitutional court order. Martin Luther King, Jr., was confronted by numerous court orders and injunctions during his 1963 through 1968 civil rights campaign. The events of the 1963 Easter weekend and the resulting trial and appeal, establish the tone and set forth the legal issues involved.

In the early 1960's the atmosphere in Birmingham, Alabama allowed whites and blacks to walk the same streets, share the same water supply and sewer system but little else. Bathrooms, taxicabs, buses, all parks and libraries were segregated. Speech was not free, telephones were tapped, mail intercepted and volunteers stood guard 24 hours a day over negro churches, Jewish synagogues, and activists' homes. There had been 22 reported bombings of negro churches and homes. Dynamite attempts were made against two large Jewish temples. In short, Birmingham repressed any civil rights activity, and public safety commissioner Eugene ("Bull") Connor with his police force were enforcers of these segregationist and repressive policies. Frequently individuals were arrested for "vagrancy" which was not a bailable offense in Birmingham. Bull Connor had no respect for federal law, the decisions of the United States Supreme Court or anyone he disagreed with. When questioned about the arrest of three negro ministers from Montgomery who were visiting Birmingham in 1958, he stated "We don't give a damn about the law. Down here we make our own law... I had them picked up on a charge of vagrancy until we could find out what they were doing here. We're not going to have outsiders coming in and stirring up trouble. If they come here and do the wrong kind of talking, they'll see the inside of our jail." When faced with a Federal District Court order desegregating the City's recreational facilities, officials closed 67 parks, 38 playgrounds and 4 golf courses thereby angering many whites who began to protest. This was the first indication that the power of Bull Connor might be weakening.

The Supreme Court school desegregation decision in 1954 (Brown v. Board of Education) ordering integration with all deliberate speed (set forth in a decision a year later) had revitalized the civil rights movement. While some border states moved to comply, deep south states such as Mississippi and Alabama refused. Their public officials made it clear they would take no action to comply with federal law. In 1961 George Wallace was elected governor of Alabama mostly based on his position that the Supreme Court "did not have the brains to try a chicken thief." To counter this the NAACP opened various offices and established branches throughout Alabama. The fight was on and the forces of desegregation were to be led by Martin Luther King, Jr., born in Atlanta, Georgia in 1929. His father was a Baptist minister and his mother a school teacher. He left Morehouse College (all negro) in 1948 with a liberal arts degree and a major in sociology. Moving north, he studied for a bachelor of divinity degree at Crozer Theological Seminary in Chester, Pennsylvania graduating first in his class. In 1951 he entered Boston University where he earned a Ph.D. in systematic theology. He accepted the position of pastor of the Dexter Avenue Baptist Church in Montgomery, Alabama. Relocating there with his wife, Coretta, in June, 1954, he quickly realized most of the diehard southern officials refused to obey the recently decided case of Brown v. Board of Education.

On December 1, 1955, a middle age black woman, Mrs. Rosa Parks, boarded a bus in Montgomery, Alabama and sat in a vacant seat in the middle section. She was a seamstress and secretary of the local NAACP chapter and she had put in a hard day at work, her feet hurt. When told she had to move to the back, she refused and was arrested. A week later Martin Luther King held an evening mass meeting at Holt Street Church attended by 4,000 Montgomery blacks. The acts of Parks and King began a long phase of attempted peaceful demonstrations.

Civil rights advocates organized a boycott of the City's transportation system which was completely effective, cutting off most of the bus company's revenues and precluding much downtown Christmas shopping. Black domestic workers could not get to work and were fired but that was quickly changed when the whites found they could not get along without them. The Klan went to work with night rides and bombings. King's home and that of Ralph Abernathy, his church and the homes of others were bombed. One honest police detective arrested two individuals for the bombing and they were indicted. In fact they even signed confessions. Despite all of this the two men were acquitted by an all white jury and walked grinning out of the courtroom.

Meanwhile, using the Federal Voting Rights Act of 1957 and 1960, blacks were registering to vote. Taking one city at a time, starting with Albany, Georgia, King committed himself to desegregating public facilities. Having obtained the support of Federal Justice Department lawyers and some federal judges, King found himself in situations where local judges enjoined his activities and much time had to be taken before federal judges overruled the state court judges. Hence he began to lose credibility with many local blacks but he did not want to alienate the Federal Justice Department and federal courts who were helping as much as they could. That is the situation King found himself in just before Easter 1963 when he was preparing for marches and demonstrations in Birmingham, Alabama. That preparation actually began in December, 1962 during a three day planning session near Savannah, Georgia. Rather than have scattered demonstrations, it was agreed that they would concentrate on the lunch counters in a large number of department stores centered in downtown Birmingham. It was known a number of these department stores, owned by nationwide chains, would be willing to desegregate if city officials would allow it. King went on a nationwide speaking tour to raise money for the demonstrations and legal costs which he knew would result.

King's lawyers filed an application for marches. Applicable law was Section 1159 of the Birmingham City Code. It required a permit for a parade or public demonstration, a written application to city commissioners stating the purpose for which the event was to be held and the places it would occur. However, if in view of the commission, the public welfare, peace, safety, health, decency, good order, morals, or convenience required the application be rejected, it would be.

The election for Birmingham mayor was held on April 2, 1963 and Albert Boutwell defeated Bull Connor. The victory resulted from a coalition of black and white moderates. The Justice Department asked

Martin Luther King, Jr., to hold off on the upcoming sit-ins at the department stores. However, pressure from his constituents caused the planning to go forward. The three city commissioners including Bull Connor announced they would take legal action and proceeded to obtain an injunction against the planned large scale demonstration on Good Friday and Easter Sunday, April 12 and 14, 1963. On April 10, attorneys Breckenridge and McBee, representing the City of Birmingham, presented State Circuit Court Judge William A. Jenkins, Jr., with an application for a temporary injunction directing the leaders of the demonstration to cease their activities. The allegation was basically that the demonstrations were "calculated to provoke breaches of peace in the city." Evidence was presented by way of affidavits showing there had already been numerous breaches of the peace. King, having been briefed by his attorneys regarding the probable unconstitutionality of the statute, knew that if they did not proceed their entire strategy would fizzle out, hence he and the other leaders decided that if an injunction was issued it would be their duty to violate it.

The leaders were concerned regarding the contempt of court weapon in the judge's possession. If criminal contempt sentences were sought the maximum was five days in jail and fines up to $50 for each offense. However if civil contempt charges were pursued they could be ordered jailed until they purged themselves of the contempt by apologizing for the violation and promising not to defy the injunction in the future. They took the calculated risk the city would not pursue civil contempt since they would not want the leaders jailed indefinitely thereby becoming martyrs, and creating sympathy for the movement. The next question was should King himself lead the demonstration and be arrested. He had not led any of the recent sit-ins or picketing demonstrations. His role had been to coordinate with local black leaders. King decided it was time he stepped to the point and go to jail. They faced two other concerns. One was their bail fund was running dry and if they opposed the injunction it would cost more money and time. They elected to ignore the injunction, and although the papers were properly served the defendants proceeded to lead the demonstrations. This lost them points with the United States Department of Justice and created in some people's minds the opinion that just as southern officials violated federal court orders and injunctions so did the demonstrators. Rather than following the law, the demonstrators also showed they could and would ignore it.

King and Abernathy led the Friday march and were arrested. King's brother, A.D. King, led more than 1,500 blacks in an Easter Sunday protest march and he too was arrested. The defense, offered by attorney Greenberg, was that never in the history of Birmingham had an application actually gone to the full city commission. It had always simply been issued by the city clerk after review by the traffic division according to no published rule or regulation. Judge Jenkins decided that the ordinance was clear and whether or not the procedure had been followed in the past, it was required, and the defendants had violated the injunction he issued. Attorney Constance Motley, on behalf of the defendants, questioned Bull Connor and established the commission had never, in its history, became involved in the issuing or refusal of any other parade permit. The Judge refused to hear any more evidence from the city, but the defendants showed the permit ordinance was administered in an arbitrary fashion. The defense called the Birmingham police chief, Jamie Moore, and he agreed the Friday and Sunday marches had been relatively peaceful and were controlled by his office without the help of outside law enforcement agencies. Evidence was introduced regarding two approaches to Bull Connor for a permit which he refused. The evidence was objected to since Connor could not bind the commission as a whole. The judge sustained the objection. To avoid being found in civil contempt a strategy was developed by defense attorneys to prepare a "statement" wherein the four defendants set forth the clarification of their position and publicly stated they had no intention of violating the law and that they would in the future urge their followers not to engage in mass picketing or congregate into mobs so as to cause breaches of the peace. Although Judge Jenkins did not accept the document into evidence he did seem to soften his position after he reviewed it. Of course the city's attorneys argued "after all, this is a government of law, it is a government of order, and if we ever get away from that, we are in chaos."

Greenberg argued the defendants' First and Fourteenth Amendment rights and citing a U.S. Supreme Court decision, contended that if an injunction was void to start with it would not be contempt to violate it, just as it would not be unlawful to violate an invalid statute. The real question was whether or not the injunction was invalid on its face and that issue was appealed to the United States Supreme Court after Judge Jenkins found the defendants were "deliberate and blatant... in their denials of the Court's authority, that there had been no apology and no indication that the defendants intended to comply with the order in the future. He sentenced each of the defendants to a fine of $50 and jail term of five days and they were allowed to go free on bond.

Although the sentences were the maximum King felt they were pretty light inasmuch as they were not found in civil contempt and he took it as a victory. Demonstrations continued in Birmingham and with the help of Justice Department attorneys a settlement was reached on May 10, 1963 which called for desegregation of lunch counters, restrooms, fitting rooms and drinking fountains; the hiring of blacks in job categories previously denied them and agreement to try and persuade city officials to release jailed demonstrators on bond or on their own recognizance. A biracial committee was formed to improve communications between whites and negroes. The agreement did not mention desegregation of the public schools. Of course, as in most agreements, there were those on each side that did not think it met their needs. King and the others went on to campaign in Selma, Alabama while the case wound its way through the Alabama appellate courts. Finally, in early 1966 a petition to the Supreme Court of the United States for writ of certiorari was filed. The petitioners asked the United States Supreme Court to review the decision of the Alabama Supreme Court upholding the contempt convictions. The title of the case was <u>Walker v. City of Birmingham</u>.

On July 2, 1964, President Lyndon B. Johnson signed the Civil Rights Act of 1964 and it, along with the work of the NAACP led by Dr. Martin Luther King, Jr., and Ralph Abernathy, revived interest throughout the United States in the issue of civil rights for blacks. During the ten years following the Civil War, blacks made great strides in the south under the administration of Republicans. That ended when Republicans, needing the support of southern Democrats to uphold the Electoral Commission decision awarding the disputed election of 1876 to republican Rutherford Hayes, agreed to reduce federal troops in the south. Subsequently, civil rights efforts ended and a U.S. Supreme Court decision in 1883 held the Civil Rights Act of 1875, forbidding racial discrimination in public accommodation facilities, unconstitutional on the basis that social contacts were private matters not subject to federal regulation. In 1896 the U.S. Supreme Court, in the famous case of <u>Plessy v. Ferguson</u> found that separate but equal facilities required by law did not deny anyone equal protection of the law. Put another way, the purposes of the Fourteenth Amendment were frustrated.

In many areas of the country when whites found blacks were using civil disobedience to pursue their agenda, a backlash occurred and the riots of 1966 occurred in Chicago, Cleveland and even in San

Francisco. Put in this context, what the U.S. Supreme Court would do in the King case was not clear. Many of the court's civil rights decisions were by a narrow margin of 5 to 4 or 6 to 3. Justice Hugo Black, a strong libertarian, had major reservations regarding protests when they involved trespass or physical acts and not pure speech. It was in this environment that the case arrived at the U.S. Supreme Court for decision in 1966.

In November of that year, the court for the first time during the 1960's upheld convictions of non-violent demonstrators. In the case of Adderley v. Florida, 32 black college students were arrested for gathering on the grounds of a county jail in Tallahassee to protest the arrest of other students who had attempted to integrate local theaters. The majority decision was written by Justice Black, who had been raised in the south, and he was supported by Clark, Holland, White and Stewart. Simply put, the court upheld the right of the state to control activities on its property. There was emphasis on the fact it was jail property and that security was a legitimate state interest.

The dissent led by Justice Douglas included Chief Justice Earl Warren, Abe Fortas and William Brennan, Jr. The essence of their argument was, "Today a trespass law was used to penalize people for exercising a constitutional right. Tomorrow a disorderly conduct statute, or a breach of the peace statute, or a vagrancy statute will be put to the same end." King's lawyers noted Justice Stewart, who would write the Walker v. City of Birmingham opinion, had joined the majority in the Adderley case. The dissenters in Adderley were the four supporters of civil rights during the 1960's in just about every case. Justice Warren was the biggest surprise since he was appointed by President Eisenhower in 1953 and was known as a strong Republican and admirer of state's rights. He was also known to believe in judicial self-restraint. However, once on the bench he found himself more comfortable with a concept of constitutional law that valued individual rights. He first reflected his views when he wrote the historic opinion in Brown v. Board of Education, a 1954 decision that resulted in President Eisenhower making the comment his appointment of Warren was the worst mistake he had ever made.

Jack Greenberg, a veteran Supreme Court arguer, presented the case for the petitioners. However, he allowed Assistant United States Solicitor General Lewis Claiborne to share his time since he was well respected by members of the Supreme Court. The federal government supported the petitioners. The case was heard on March 13, 1967.

Greenberg had started to present his argument when he was interrupted by Justice Holland who asked Greenberg to address himself to the pivotal issue, the 'question of adequate state grounds…" This was the weakest part of the petitioners case inasmuch as the ordinance was clear and the petitioners had been advised both verbally and in writing that they were required to obtain a permit by presenting an application to the entire commission. Of course Greenberg argued that was not the way it was done in Birmingham. However Justice Stewart pointed out the law was clear and it was he who on June 12, 1967 announced the decision of the court.

Using established law he stated the validity of an injunction cannot be challenged in a contempt proceeding. He differentiated between one's right to not follow an unconstitutional law as versus one's right not to follow what one believes to be an unconstitutional court order. He pointed out that before violating the injunction petitioners did not exercise their right to challenge the trial court's order in the Alabama state courts and that petitioners bypassed the orderly judicial review of the injunction in Alabama's courts. Instead, they proceeded to deliberately violate the injunction, no doubt expecting they would go to jail. Chief Justice Earl Warren joined by Justice Douglas and

Justice Brennan dissented from the majority stating the real issue was Birmingham officials doing everything possible to frustrate the parade permit process and discriminate against petitioners. They believed the heart of the case was missed by the majority and stated it to be "…. a parade-permit ordinance vesting of total unfettered discretion in city officials made it patently unconstitutional." They attacked the majority's statement that obedience to a court injunction is always necessary to preserve respect for courts and law,

Justice Warren stated "I do not believe that giving this court's seal of approval to such a gross misuse of the judicial process is likely to lead to greater respect for the law any more than it is likely to lead to greater protection for First Amendment freedoms. The ex parte temporary injunction has a long and odious history in this country, and its susceptibility to misuse is all too apparent from the facts of the case."

Justice Douglas' position was that an ordinance, unconstitutional on its face or patently unconstitutional as applied, is not made sacred by an unconstitutional injunction that enforces it. His position was that "courts as well as citizens are not free to ignore all the procedures of the law. The constitutional freedom of which the court speaks can be won only if judges honor the constitution."

Justice Brennan rendered a harsh dissent referring to the negroes' having to exercise respect for state judicial process as being extortion, elevating a state rule of judicial administration above the right of peaceful demonstration and free expression, guaranteed by the federal constitution. He pointed out the majority opinion lets loose a devastatingly destructive weapon for suppression of cherished freedoms believed indispensable to the maintenance of our free society. He believed there was an inversion of values with the majority using established law dealing with federal labor policy (Mine Workers Case) to support the clearly unconstitutional injunction and parade permit law. He concluded with the following statement: "To preach, 'respect for judicial process' in this context," said Brennan, "is to deny the right to speak at all."

On October 30, 1967, Martin Luther King, Jr., and the other three petitioners returned to Birmingham to serve their five day sentence for contempt of court. King told reporters this was not his first time in jail, actually by this time it was his 19[th.] The weather was poor and he developed a viral infection resulting in his release a day early. In 1968, just a few months before Robert Kennedy was assassinated, Dr. Martin Luther King, Jr., was shot and killed by James Earl Ray. In 1973, Bull Connor died of a heart attack.

Presently, in the south, African Americans vote and insure their proper representation in local and state government. Federal policies often favor minorities in an attempt to grant them equal opportunities under the law. No government can legislate away prejudice and although many cultures of color have assimilated into the diverse and complex society of the United States, African Americans continue to be disadvantaged by what is offered and what they can make of it. All must continue to improve this situation even if it takes many more generations, to effect real change for the better.

CHAPTER 8

TRIAL OF EZRA POUND

AMERICAN POET, AUTHOR AND translator, Ezra Pound was born in Hailey, Idaho in 1885. At 20 years of age he left the United States to reside in Europe, mostly in Great Britain, before moving to Italy in the late 1930s. Marrying in England, his wife, Dorothy, subsequently gave up her British citizenship to become a citizen of the United States. She did not actually live in this country until after World War II when Ezra Pound was confined. Beginning in 1912 and continuing to his death in 1972, he was considered a world-class poet. During World War II Pound lived in Italy and was on the payroll of the Italian government broadcasting negative radio messages about the governments of the United States and Great Britain. Interestingly, his messages were not specifically about the war. He was particularly acrimonious regarding economic issues and vehemently anti-Semitic alleging Jewish dominance of financial markets. Surrendering to American troops in May 1945 he was incarcerated at a military prison in Pisa, Italy. He remained there for seven months and was treated much differently than other prisoners. Since he was an American citizen and considered a traitor, he was put in a cage in the middle of the prison without protection from the weather. He had been considered an eccentric prior to his incarceration but it appears his seven months in a cage caused deterioration in his mental state. When he was brought to the United States in November 1945, he was indicted, for the second time, on charges of treason relating to his radio broadcasts. He thought he was brought to this country to help our government plan for the future of Europe. This distorted thinking was considered one of the bases for psychiatrists finding he was somewhat delusional.

Apparently, it was uncontroverted that he did not truly understand he was charged with treason, but if found competent to aid in his defense, he would stand trial for treason. The defendant refused to acknowledge he was insane, hence he could not defend against the treason charge on that basis. This gave rise to interesting legal issues which his attorney realized early on had the potential of creating a situation in which Pound would be confined, possibly for many years, even though he was presumed innocent and never brought to trial. The allegations of his treason did not quite put him in the same category as Lord Haw Haw, Axis Sally, or Tokyo Rose, since he was not an entertainer, did not deal with military matters and apparently did not really care whether anyone listened to him. There was a real question as to whether or not he, in fact, gave "aid and comfort to the enemy" or was simply critical of the government, particularly President Roosevelt and the alleged "Jewish conspiracy". In fact, his broadcasts were somewhat boring and unenlightening. Because of his celebrity as a literary genius he may well have been found innocent of the treason charges had he actually ever been tried. He, in fact, spent slightly more time in confinement than Tokyo Rose since Pound was not released until 1958 at which time he returned to Italy with his wife.

During the years of his confinement at St. Elizabeth's Hospital (which at that time was operated by the National Security Agency as a mental facility), he was precluded from bringing his assets from Italy into the United States because of provisions of the Alien Property Act. On the one hand, he was being charged with treason because he was a U.S. citizen and on the other he was treated as an alien. Another strange anomaly was he was given a prestigious Library of Congress award in 1949 known as the Bollingen Prize which resulted in a payment of $1,000 made to him by the United States Treasury. Although there were some objections to the prize, United States literary luminaries felt he was deserving of it. Also, at that time a man named Bennett Cerf was the publisher of Random House and he refused to publish an anthology of 12 poems by Mr. Pound in the publication *Modern Library*. This created quite a stir and subsequently Pound's poems were included in the work and he was paid $300.

In October 1945 the Grand Jury of the District Court of the United States for the District of Columbia returned an indictment alleging "Ezra Pound at Rome, Italy and in other places within the Kingdom of Italy and outside any particular state or district but within the jurisdiction of the United States and of this Court, being the district in which he was found and into which he was first brought, continuously and at all times beginning on the 11 ʰ day of December 1941 and continuing through May 3, 1945, while a citizen of the United States and therefore owing personal allegiance to the United States, knowingly, intentionally, willfully, unlawfully, feloniously, traitorously and treasonably did adhere to the enemies of the United States, to wit; the Kingdom of Italy and the military allies of said Kingdom of Italy, with which the United States at all times since December 11, 1941 have been at war, giving to the said enemies of the United States aid and comfort." It was further alleged he accepted employment from the Kingdom of Italy as a radio propagandist and was paid money for his work. The indictment went on to allege specific instances of radio broadcasts and money paid.

Treason is the only crime specifically set forth in the Constitution of the United States. Article Ill, Section 3, States, "Treason against the United States, shall consist only in levering war against them, or in adhering to their enemies, giving them aid and comfort. No person shall be convicted of treason unless on the Testimony of two Witnesses to the same overt Act, or on confession in open Court."

The definition of the crime of treason at that time contained in the United States Criminal Code was as follows: "Treason. Whoever, owing allegiance to the United States, levies war against them or adheres to their enemies, giving them aid and comfort within the United States or elsewhere, is guilty of treason."

The punishment for treason includes death, imprisonment of not less than five years and a fine of not less than $10,000. Admission to bail is expressly permitted by Federal statute in all capital offenses of which treason is one.

"Bail may be admitted upon all arrests in criminal cases where the punishment may be death; but in such case it shall be taken only by the Supreme Court or a Circuit Court, or by a justice of the Supreme Court, a circuit judge, or judge of a district court, who shall exercise their discretion therein, having regard to the nature and circumstances of the offense, and of the evidence, and to the usages of law." Hence, a defendant accused of treason may be allowed to bail while awaiting trial within the discretion of the court. Judge Laws refused to release the defendant on bail.

On February 13, 1946, the one-day trial to determine if Pound could aid in his defense commenced before a jury. There were four witnesses called, all well-known psychiatrists. Dr. Wendell Munci of Johns Hopkins found Pound to be "paranoid" in the sense that he engaged in delusions and self-aggrandizement. Dr. Marion R. King, Chief Medical Officer for the Bureau of Prisons and of the Public

Health Service, found Pound easily distractible. This precluded Pound from pursuing a logical conversation in a reasonable manner. He was easily sidetracked and roamed from subject to unconnected subject. He felt it would be very difficult for him to aid in his own defense by conferring with his attorney. Dr. Joseph L. Gilbert was the chief psychiatrist at Gallinger Municipal Hospital where Pound was confined during the first few months after his return to the United States and before he was transferred to St. Elizabeth's. He referred to Pound's grandiose ideas and his higher-than-average I.Q. (but which was not in the area of genius) and felt he was suffering from paranoia.

Although the witnesses were cross-examined by government lawyers, it was apparent they were engaging in a perfunctory effort because some of the psychiatrists testifying actually worked for the government and one was appointed by Judge Laws. The jury took a short time to return the verdict of "unsound mind". In this situation the Court could only order Pound to be confined at St. Elizabeth's until he was of sound mind sufficient to aid his lawyers in defending him. His attorney, Mr. Cornel, realized he could be confined for many years, still not convicted of a crime, but continuing to be under indictment. The law did not provide for a specific remedy in this situation. He felt Judge Laws had the inherent power, which he did, to order Pound's release should it be determined he would never be of sufficiently sound mind to aid in his defense. Between 1946 and 1958 motions were brought using the mechanism of a writ of habeas corpus but he was not released until Judge Laws dismissed the indictment on April 18, 1958, finding upon the affidavit of Dr. Wilfred Oberholser, the fourth psychiatrist who testified at the trial and who was superintendent of St. Elizabeth's Hospital, that the defendant was incompetent to stand trial and that there was no likelihood his condition would improve in the foreseeable future. Interestingly, the Court also commented that the defense also had available to it psychiatric testimony suggesting there was a strong probability that the commission of the crimes charged was the result of insanity and it appeared the government was not in a position to challenge this medical testimony. Hence, the government did not oppose the motion to dismiss. This bargain was obviously an agreement by all involved to terminate the case in the interest of justice.

The 72-year-old poet returned to Italy with members of his family including his wife, Dorothy, who lived in Washington, D.C. during the years of his confinement and who visited him regularly. Actually, although Pound was initially confined at St. Elizabeth's in a barred ward, he was moved to better accommodations in 1946 since it appeared the prison-type atmosphere was causing his condition to worsen. He was never considered an escape threat and he had the support of numerous well-known literary figures including some in government such as Sherman Adams, Assistant to President Eisenhower.

This case illustrates the distinction between an individual being incompetent to stand trial and the insanity defense in a trial. It also is an early example of a U.S. citizen being apprehended in another country and being returned to this country to stand trial. A more recent example would be the case of John Walker Lindh. The use of psychiatric testimony is well illustrated and the power of it must be appreciated because if it is admitted, uncontroverted, juries and judges have no practical choice but to accept it. Finally, the concept of knowing right from wrong, which is the bottom line of an insanity defense in a trial for a specific crime, is in fact different from the issue of a person being of sound mind so as to be able to aid his attorney in his defense. Being a United States citizen, Pound had the right to counsel and the right to prove his incarceration in Italy for seven months after the war negatively affected his mental state so as to be a factor in his competency to stand trial. This gives food for thought in incarcerations of United

States' citizens who are being treated as unlawful combatants during time of war. The failure of the government to provide U.S. citizens their Constitutional right to a speedy trial indicates a policy exists that treats their alleged crimes as being more heinous than treason. Some would argue the present terrorist threat is more serious than that posed by Pound but should seriousness of the threat abrogate Constitutional rights possessed by citizens of the United States? Most would respond in the negative.

However, there is ample legal precedence for U.S. citizens to be tried by the military in time of war, insurrection or when marshal law is declared. Examples are Captain H. Wyrz, the Commander of Andersonville Prison during the Civil War and those convicted in the plot to assassinate President Abraham Lincoln. More modern examples are two U.S. citizens who fought for Germany during World War II and who were landed by Nazi submarine on Long Island, New York to commit sabotage. Later captured, they were tried and convicted by a military court. The case of Jose Padilla, who is a U.S. Citizen "captured" as an enemy combatant in 2002, was to go before the U.S. Supreme Court. He had been held in a military prison in the United States for over three years. Originally seized because of his alleged involvement in a "dirty bomb plot", the U.S. Government decided to try him in civilian court for violating criminal law based on his alleged fighting for the enemy in Afghanistan. Padilla opposed the transfer of his case to civilian courts but was unsuccessful. He was tried, convicted and sentenced to 21 years in federal prison. This is a similar sentence imposed on John Walker Lindh who was convicted of terrorism because he acted as a foot soldier for the Taliban in Afghanistan and who could be released in the near future, having served most of sentence.

CHAPTER 9

THE NUREMBERG TRIAL

AT THE CONCLUSION OF World War II, numerous trials were
held in different parts of the world to deal with those alleged to have
committed atrocities and war crimes. Only the highest leadership of the
Nazi party was tried at Nuremberg. Many others were tried in German
courts and a number were executed. A German general, Dostert, was
shot for ordering the killing of United States soldiers held as prisoners
in 1944. General Yamashita Tomoyuki and General Homma Masaharu
were sentenced to death in Manila on December 7, 1945 for numerous
atrocities and war crimes. The commandants of Dachau and Belsen
concentration camps were executed and thousands of others were tried
in both Europe and Asia.

However, the longest trial and the one most widely followed was in
Nuremberg before eight justices, two each from the four allied powers
(United States, Great Britain, Russia and France). The prosecution's
case extended from November 20, 1945 until March 4, 1946. The
defense case then continued until May 1946. Following is a list of
defendants and some information regarding their backgrounds. Of the
22 defendants, 10 were executed in September 1946, three exonerated

and seven served prison sentences. One, Herman Goring, committed suicide just before he was to be executed.

Martin Bormann (1900-1945) was an early Nazi party member who eventually rose to Chief of Cabinet in the Office of Deputy Fuhrer Rudolph Hess. When Hess flew to Scotland in 1941, Bormann took his position as head of the party. He was a close confidante of Hitler and controlled access to him. He was anti-Semitic, anti-Slav, and anti-Christian. He was in Hitler's bunker during the final days of the war and witnessed Hitler's marriage and suicide. It is thought he was killed while trying to leave Berlin; however, some felt he escaped and lived in South America. He was formerly pronounced dead by a German court in 1973. Having been tried in absentia, he was convicted and sentenced to death by hanging.

Karl Doenitz (1891-1980) was a naval officer from 1910 through 1945 and served on virtually all types of ships in the German Navy. In 1935 he was given command of German submarines and during World War II his U-boats sunk over 20,000,000 tons of allied shipping. In 1943 he became a Grand Admiral and succeeded Raeder as Supreme Commander of the German Navy. In his last order Hitler appointed him Supreme Commander of the German Armed Forces. He was found guilty and sentenced to 10 years imprisonment. His was actually the lightest sentence except for the three who were acquitted.

Hans Frank (1900-1946) was a storm trooper-lawyer in Munich during the 1920's. He served as Minister of Justice of Bavaria, Reich Minister of Justice and was Governor-General of Poland after it was occupied. In 1942 he called for return to constitutional law in Germany and was stripped of his party affiliation and offices. He was sentenced to death by hanging.

Wilhelm Frick (1877-1946), educated as a lawyer, became a Munich police officer and connected with Hitler in the 1920's when he became a

Nazi deputy in the Reichstag. He subsequently lost control of the police to Himmler but he drafted and controlled much of the Nazi legislation which was used against Hitler's opposition. During World War II he was the protector of Bohemia and Moravia. He was sentenced to death by hanging.

Hans Fritzscht (1900-1953), a student of history, became the head of the German radio news service in 1932. He joined the Nazi party and controlled the Press Section of the Reich Ministry of Propaganda. During World War II he served in senior positions at the Propaganda Ministry. He was acquitted.

Walther Funk (1890-1960), journalist with a financial background, was Hitler's personal economic adviser. After serving in the Propaganda Ministry he became the Reich Minister of Economics. He also served as President of the Reich Bank and was a member of the Central Planning Commission during World War II He was sentenced to life imprisonment.

Hermann Goering (1893-1946) was probably the most famous of the defendants and the one who caused Justice Jackson severe distress on cross-examination. He was a decorated war hero in World War I. He was credited with the downing of 22 allied aircraft and ended his service as Commander of the Reichthofen Squadron, the most famous of the German air squadrons. In 1928 he was elected to the Reichstag becoming its President in 1932. After Hitler became Chancellor in 1933, Goering became the Minister of Interior of Prussia with control over its police forces. He established concentration camps and was heavily involved in reducing the civil rights and press freedoms of the German populous. He became Commander in Chief of the Air Force in 1935 and was named Hitler's successor in 1939 as Chairman of the Reich Council. He directed the air war campaigns but gave up too early trying to destroy the British Air Force switching to bombing English cities such as London, giving the British Air Forces an opportunity to increase their numbers. The air war failures in Russia added to his decline in power and just before Hitler's death, Goering was stripped of all offices and placed under arrest. Hitler's will stipulated Goering was expelled from the Nazi party. Although he was sentenced to death by hanging, Goering managed to commit suicide shortly before he was to be executed.

Rudolph Hess (1894-1987) served as Hitler's private secretary from 1925 to 1932 and they enjoyed a close relationship. He was made Deputy Party Leader in 1933 and just as World War II started he became a member of the Council for Reich's Defense as well as the Cabinet Council. In 1939 he was declared the successor to Hitler and Goering, although Hitler never thought he would actually serve. Inexplicably he decided to fly to Scotland in 1941 where he bailed out of his plane and tried to visit the Duke of Hamilton with whom he had a previous acquaintance. No doubt somewhat deluded, his intention was to try to persuade the British government Hitler was friendly and had peaceful intentions. Knowing war with both Russia and Britain could end up in disaster, he hoped to arrange a truce with Great Britain so as to be able to defeat Russia. His delusions were fed by the British Intelligence Services. He was imprisoned and after trial at Nuremberg he was sentenced to life imprisonment. Hess was to become the last surviving prisoner at the allied prison known as Spandau. Built to house 600 prisoners, after the war it held 7 and gradually they were all released except Hess. Although the four powers had monthly meetings to discuss conditions at the prison and rotate the guards, the Russians refused to allow Hess to be released and he committed suicide at Spandau in July 1987.

Alfred Jodl (1890-1947), a descendant of a long line of soldiers, became Chief of Operations of the German Army in 1939. He worked subordinately to Hitler and Keitel during the war but his relationship with Hitler was difficult. His attempts to obtain a front line position were continually denied. He was wounded along with Hitler during a July 1944 assassination attempt when a bomb exploded during a meeting. He was sentenced to death by hanging.

Ernst Kaltenbrunner (1903-1946), a lawyer, joined the Austrian Nazi Party in 1932. He was arrested twice in 1934 and 1935, charged with conspiracy. Subsequently he commanded the SS, became the Austrian Minister for State Security, and in 1941 Lieutenant-General of Police. After Heydrich was assassinated in 1943 he headed the Reich Main Security Office which oversaw the Gestapo, criminal police, and as of 1944 the Military Intelligence Service known as Abwehr. He was the senior individual responsible for the concentration camp system and the extermination of the Jews. He was sentenced to death by hanging.

Wilhelm Keitel (1882-1946), a professional military officer, served in various high positions in the 1930's and became Chief of the Staff of the High Command of the Armed Forces with the rank of Colonel General. He became a field marshal in 1940 and reported directly to Hitler. He was sentenced to death by hanging.

Constantin Freiherr von Neurath (1873-1956) was the Nazi Foreign Minister in 1937 but shortly thereafter he was fired and replaced by Ribbentrop. He became President of the Secretary Cabinet Council, was Administer Without Portfolio and had membership on the Council for Reich Defense. Most of these positions were honorary. He became the protector of Bohemia and Moravia in 1939, however he was considered lenient and in 1941 was put on permanent sick leave. He was sentenced to 15 years imprisonment.

Franz von Papen (1879-1969) who served as a military officer in World War I, became a diplomat and military attaché in Mexico and Washington. In 1932, without a majority in the Reichstag he served as Chancellor and his policies helped the Nazis come to power. Subsequently he became Hitler's Vice-Chancellor, served as President of Prussia and Ambassador to Austria. However during World War II he was demoted and served in the embassy in Ankara, Turkey. He was one of the three defendants who were acquitted.

Erich Raeder (1876-1960), serving in the Germany Navy after 1894, rose in rank to become Chief of the Naval Command in 1928. As the Second World War progressed, Raeder's arguments with Hitler over strategy and his failure to stop convoys supplying Russia caused him to resign in 1943. He was sentenced to life imprisonment.

Joachin von Ribbentrop (1893-1946) joined the Nazi party in 1932 and became Hitler's adviser on foreign affairs. He helped negotiate the change in power from Papen to Hitler. After serving for a period as Ambassador to London, he returned to become Foreign Minister in 1938. He negotiated the Nazi-Soviet pact allowing Hitler to invade Poland without Soviet interference. In fact, much of Eastern Poland was then turned over to the Soviets. He served as Foreign Minister until the end of the war. He was sentenced to death by hanging.

Alfred Rosenberg (1893-1946) who was a very early member of the Nazi party (1919) led the party while Hitler was imprisoned. However, he was a poor leader and the party degenerated. Although he had ambitions to be a leader in international relations, the best position he obtained was in the Nazi Foreign Affairs Department where his responsibility was contact with fascist organizations abroad. He did serve as Minister for Occupied Eastern Territories and was involved with the extermination of the Jews. He was against the extermination of Slavs although his views were ignored. He was sentenced to death by hanging.

Fritz Sauckel (1894-1946), another early member of the Nazi party (1923), became the Thuringian Minister of the Interior and then

Governor with a seat in the Reichstag. Between 1942 and 1945 he was in charge of labor mobilization. He was sentenced to death by hanging.

Hjalmar Schacht (1877-1970) was raised in the United States, returned to Germany and studied economics. He became a Banker and Reich Currency Commissioner and between 1923 and 1930 headed the Reich Bank. Resentful that Germany had to make reparation payments after World War I, he encouraged Hitler and raised money for his election in an attempt to rejuvenate nationalism. He held various high positions in the Ministry of Economics and again headed the Reich Bank beginning in 1938. He was arrested after the July bomb plot in 1944 and spent the last months of the war in various concentration camps. He was acquitted.

Baldur von Schirach (1907-1974), an early party member, spent most of the years before World War II leading Hitler youth movements. By 1936 he had six million members which increased to almost eight million in 1938. In 1940 he enlisted in the Army and ultimately became Governor of Vienna. He complained about the mistreatment of Slavs and Jews but he remained in office until the end of the war. He was sentenced to 20 years.

Arthur Seyss-Inquart (1892-1946), another lawyer, was wounded in the First World War and thereafter practiced law in Vienna. In 1931 he became a member of the Austrian Nazi Party. He became Austrian Minister of Interior and helped create the "crisis" that allowed Hitler to invade Austria. The day after he became Chancellor of Austria, German troops marched in. From 1940 through 1945, he was Reich Commissioner of the Netherlands. Hitler named him in his will as Foreign Minister but he never took the position. He was sentenced to death by hanging.

Albert Speer (1905-1981), an architect and Nazi Party member beginning in 1931, became one of Hitler's favorites and designed numerous structures that allegedly would last a thousand years. During World War II, he served in various administrative posts and ultimately became Head of War Production. He was sentenced to 20 years in imprisonment.

Julius Streicher (1885-1946) was vehemently anti-Semitic, an early Nazi Party member (1921), Governor of Bavaria and a member of the Reichstag. He published the newspaper, Der Sturmer, and continually attacked Jews. Because of this, Hitler made him Director of the Central Committee for the Defense Against Jewish Atrocity. He prospered through the sale of newspapers and expropriation of Jewish property. He was considered obscene, sadistic and corrupt even by Nazi Party standards and when Hitler received strong complaints, Streicher was dismissed from his Party posts in 1940. He was sentenced to death by hanging.

Perhaps the most serious dilemma regarding the impaneling of the judges for what became known as the Nuremberg Trial was the question of whether or not the defendants could receive a fair trial. Many felt that if the trial could not be readily seen as being fair and in the interests of justice that it would be better to simply execute a number of the defendants as war criminals. The next decision was who would be included as defendants. The British wanted few defendants to ensure a quick trial. Their list contained ten names including Hess, however, it was questionable as to whether or not Hess was fit to stand trial since he had been under the care of British psychiatrists after landing in Scotland in 1941. At the Potsdam Conference, Stalin was insistent Hess be brought to trial because he knew Hess had tried to get the British out of the war freeing Germany to invade Russia. On the other hand, the Americans wanted to put the whole Nazi regime, dating from 1933, on trial. For example, the British did not want to try Admiral Doenitz because they felt the German Navy had avoided committing atrocities and the British Naval High Command did not like trying admirals. Eventually the list was narrowed down to those already mentioned and a number of others were listed for a second trial. With publication of the defendants list on August 29, 1945, grave precedents were set. For the first time leaders of the state were tried for starting a war and breaking treaties. Put another way, there was great concern that henceforth the victors would try the vanquished.

Meanwhile, millions of documents were being reviewed. The German propensity to keep exact records and the allies' ability to capture them resulted in literally millions of relevant documents. For instance, the complete records of the German Navy and most of the records of the Foreign Ministry were secured. The logistics were horrendous not only to review the documents, but to set up facilities at Nuremberg to actually house the hundreds of people involved in the trial. This was, in fact, the first "complex litigation." Nuremberg was a bombed out city and when the justices arrived they found themselves without bathrooms, without running water and in the case of the British, without liquor, the latter situation being promptly remedied-even so, not a good scenario for a great trial.

The indictment was agreed upon and issued on October 6, 1945. While the early British draft was only two and a half pages long, the final version, mostly because of American input, was 65 pages. The indictment contained four counts. Count one dealt with common plan or conspiracy and it covered all crimes. Count two centered on crimes against the peace and breaking treaties. Counts three and four concerned crimes against humanity and were quite detailed. For the first time the word genocide was introduced. All those subsequently found guilty were convicted of one of the two counts alleging crimes against humanity, except Hess, who was convicted of counts one and two.

While the prosecutors were responsible for policy during the time of indictment, thereafter the judges took control and had to develop procedures based on their experiences which were entirely different. There were real questions regarding what law should apply. Judge Frances Biddle (the United States Attorney General) was particularly concerned that the indictments charge a violation of law that existed before the defendants' alleged acts. In other words, that there be no ex post facto law involved. There was a question regarding "conspiracy" which was an Anglo-American theory and not necessarily applicable in an international court or against German defendants since conspiracy was not a crime in Germany. However, European law did recognize the basic principle of nulla poena or nullum crimen sine lege, there can be no punishment or indeed crime without previously declared law. The result was the prosecution had to prove violation of prior existing law in order to prove a defendant's guilt for a specified act or acts.

The trial began on November 20, 1945. The judges and prosecutors gave opening statements. On the second day the defendants had to plead and although Goering tried to give a speech he was forced to simply plead not guilty. The speech which he subsequently gave to the press basically stated that he accepted political responsibility for his own acts and the orders he issued. He rejected the concept that his acts could be described as criminal, denounced the idea that he could be responsible for others' acts which were unknown to him and which he did not approve, and refused to recognize the jurisdiction of the court, claiming he should be tried in a German court. Saddam Hussein and most other deposed heads of state accused of atrocities have argued the same points.

The lead U.S. prosecutor, Justice Robert Jackson on leave from the U.S. Supreme Court, then began the opening statement for the prosecution. Much of the speech dealt with the conspiracy charges which the Americans were responsible for proving in court. He described the Nazis as being a group of premeditated, organized criminals who conspired to wage what he called the greatest of all crimes, aggressive war. Justice Jackson outlined the Nazi strategy of taking over Germany and then the rest of Europe by exterminating enemies and controlling financiers and industrialists and then using them to produce war material. The Nazis seized Austria by trick, Czechoslovakia by bullying, and when neither worked for Poland they waged war. He produced high level documents which stated success in war can only be achieved if the war is carried out without attention to international law. Jackson's opening statement was delivered with passion, was all encompassing and was an excellent overall summary of events leading to the war and the atrocities committed during the war. As the trial continued, documents were produced that debunked the idea that Germany was forced into a war for self-defense and it became clear it was an aggressive war for the purpose of control and expansion. Some of the defendants reacted negatively to evidence when it was produced claiming a lack of knowledge and in some instances appeared horrified themselves.

When the prosecution produced a film, found by the allies, depicting a concentration camp and showing an endless river of white bodies flowing through the screen, huge piles of corpses, open common graves, etc., most of the defendants became very upset. Only Streicher seemed to agree with it. Less than half of the defense attorneys showed up for the showing of the film since they had been given the opportunity to see it the night before. A number of the defendants denied knowing such things occurred. The film set the tone of the trial, that of dead seriousness and it alerted the world to the Holocaust.

Early in the trial an attempt was made to release Hess on the basis he was incompetent. The same arguments were used regarding Krupp, an industrialist, who did not stand trial because of very poor health. Also legal arguments were made along the lines of inability to cooperate with counsel and not being able to give evidence or confront witnesses. Because Hess had feigned a loss of memory while in custody in England and had refused medical treatment which would have helped his condition, but mostly because of the unanimity of the defense experts who examined Hess and who expressed the opinion he was sane, the judges continued with the trial against him.

The pause to deal with the Hess matter interrupted the prosecution's rhythm and to return to it they called Major General Erwin Lahousen, a former Austrian Army Intelligence Officer. As the Assistant to Admiral Canaris, head of Germany Military Intelligence (ABWEHR), he attended numerous meetings and took notes for Admiral Canaris including conferences with Hitler, Keitel and numerous others. He was personal proof of orders and policies which were so shameful they had not been committed to paper even by the Nazis. He described Hitler's tricks to invade Poland such as dressing German troops in Polish uniforms and then having the phony Polish troops attack German installations, plotting the assassination of the French Generals Weygand and Giraud, causing an uprising in the Ukraine as an excuse for the wholesale slaughter of Jews, and the killing of Russian prisoners of war as policy. On cross-examination, he was asked why he did not complain regarding these policies at the time and he stated he had done so to Admiral Canaris who he claimed frequently blocked orders and sabotaged Hitler's policies. Canaris was executed by Hitler because of his involvement in the July 1944 plot to assassinate him. Lahousen's testimony directly implicated a number of the defendants including Ribbentrop who stated, "What shall I do?" after the testimony. Some of the defendants were amazed to learn that the July 1944 bomb was hatched at the Offices of Military Intelligence.

Evidence was then presented dealing with the crimes against humanity counts. This included letters between Sauchel and Rosenberg regarding forced labor. There was evidence about operation of the concentration camps which included individual evidence against each defendant directly involving him in one or more of the counts charged. As the days of December progressed, the evidence piled on and the defendants were dismayed there was so much of it and that their counsel could not refute it.

All was not perfect in the United States prosecution case. A number of prosecutors became so involved in the details and massive amounts of evidence that they did not present it well. However, at the end the American case improved with the introduction of high ranking Nazi officers who personally testified regarding their involvement in criminal acts. For example, Otto Ohlendorff, the number three man in the Gestapo, stated that between 1941 and 1942, in Russia, he led a group that directed the killing of 90,000 people. He was one of the many who testified he was "carrying out orders." He found that shooting individuals was less stressful on the soldiers than unloading bodies from gas vans. A witness named Alois Hollriegel was produced who, because he was unemployed, joined the SS. He described watching men worked to death in stone quarries, others being dropped 100 feet off cliffs as a punishment, as well as additional atrocities. A witness named Blaha, a Czech doctor and Dachau inmate, described executions at Dachau during 1943 and personally saw Bormann, Frick, Rosenberg, Funk, Sauckel and Kaltenbrunner visit the concentration camp. This caused much stress for those defendants and although there was a lively crossexamination, the doctor's testimony was accepted, since he was in the position to know because of his numerous autopsies on those beaten or shot to death.

Presentation of the American case caused problems for the other allied powers. Justice Jackson in his attempt to prove conspiracy presented a wide ranging case, using much evidence that the other prosecution teams, who were trying to prove specific acts, wanted to use. The Charter setting up the tribunal called for an expeditious trial without cumulative and redundant evidence. Not wanting to be totally minimalized, Shawcross, the lead prosecutor for Great Britain, actually presented some of his case regarding specific acts of aggression during Jackson's case pertaining to waging aggressive war. These two concepts may seem to be the same but they are actually different. The waging of aggressive war dealt with the political and overall policies of the Nazis, whereas the British intended to prove specific acts of aggression.

Shawcross was interested in the importance of the trial in developing international law, however he, being an excellent pragmatic barrister, dispassionately applied the law as it existed to specific acts. He claimed the Charter had simply laid out the procedures and aims of the tribunal and did not affect existing law. He referred to various existing international agreements and treaties, calculating there had been 99, on which to base the body of law used by the tribunal. He argued Germany had knowingly signed and accepted these international obligations and must accept an international judgment as well as the necessary punishment as a consequence of breaking them. He used Germany's invasion of Poland, Norway, Denmark, the Netherlands, Greece, Yugoslavia, and Russia as examples of Germany's violation of specific treaties involving those countries, as well as pacts such as the Locarno Pact, the Peace of Paris Pact, and others. He showed a pattern wherein the more Hitler feigned peace and the more Ribbentrop tried to negotiate specific agreements with countries, the closer the invasion became. He introduced documents showing, while negotiating these pacts, Hitler planned for aggressive war against these countries. The British presented a clear and convincing case quickly because they deliberately kept it simple. Their only real hurdle was convincing the tribunal to accept the view that treaties make international law.

Once that concept was accepted, the evidence was clearly and simply presented. Contrasting the American and the British cases, the American case concentrated on conspiracy which dealt with generalities, hence it was somewhat vague; whereas the British case dealt with specifics using evidence and events that could not be contested. Interestingly, although most everyone appeared pleased with the presentation, the Danes filed a protest with the British Foreign Office because they did not believe the case regarding the invasion of Denmark was sufficiently presented.

The British were responsible for the presentation of the individual cases against Ribbentrop and Papen (the diplomats) and the soldiers, Keitel and Jodl. They also took on the sailors, Raeder and Doenitz, although they did not have any enthusiasm for the prosecution of Doenitz who was a defendant because of American insistence. The British felt that Doenitz did not have high enough rank until 1943, was not involved in the planning of the war, nor was he personally involved in Hitler's strategy, and did not have high standing in Nazi circles, notwithstanding Hitler designating him as his successor in his will. It was thought this latter act was done in an effort to unite the various fractions in Germany as the war ended. The only real evidence against Doenitz was the Laconia Order issued by him in September 1942, stating no attempt should be made to rescue survivors of ships which were sunk. Although seemingly harsh, and applying to not only combatants but women and children, the Germans claimed this mirrored the indiscriminant allied bombing of Germany. The order did not explicitly state survivors were to be killed. However, it was argued it encouraged such activity and in fact there were some instances wherein U-boat commanders did order the shooting of survivors. Attorney Kranzbuehler, representing Doenitz, made the greatest inroads into the allied case, although his victories were minor. He knew more about naval warfare legal principles than the British (he was a German naval officer) and established through witnesses it was not illegal to attack rescue ships.

On January 17, 1946, the French Chief Prosecutor, de Menthon, gave France's opening statement. He himself had been a politician and a member of the Resistance. He concentrated on the law of war crimes and crimes against humanity. He pointed out that the transfer of judicial power by individual states to the tribunal was intentional and allowable under international law. He held the German people, as a whole, responsible for Nazi war crimes. After his opening statement he left to take up his position as French Minister of Justice and was replaced by Champetier de Ribes who had escaped from a German prison and had lived with the Resistance. de Ribes oversaw the admission of 800 documents out of 21,000 documents which were submitted during the trial. Nearly all the documents were German and very specific. They told of theft and destruction. It was explained that in France alone over 10 times the amount of money the Germans could legally take to pay occupation forces was actually stolen. Whole factories, animals, land, and train stock had been seized. The evidence helped explain why Europe was destitute. Unfortunately, this detailed examination which also included other countries and was sometimes redundant made the judges unhappy, but the Russians who planned to do exactly the same urged the Americans and the British not to interfere. While the French evidence was important it was presented dispassionately and became boring. Whereas emotion could have been put into the proof of a Nazi system in Denmark known as "compensatory" murders which meant five Danes were to be killed for every German murdered, it was developed that in fact the result was actually only about one to one. It was proved 250,000 French were deported as forced laborers. A witness described allied soldiers being beaten to death in camps. At

Mauthausen 400 prisoners were killed simply because the camp became over crowded.

In February 1946 the Russian case began. It was said Goering was looking forward to it since he thought he would be important. Roman Rudenko, the Chief Russian Prosecutor, presented evidence of the destruction by the Nazis of thousands of churches, villages, industrial establishments, hospitals, schools and libraries and established 25,000,000 people were now homeless. The number of animals killed were in the hundreds of millions. The Russians were redundant since they again put on evidence of Nazi plans for aggression, previously introduced by Justice Jackson. They then presented a surprise witness, Field Marshal Paulus, the Commander of the German Sixth Army which surrendered at Stalingrad. He was classified as a prisoner of war, not a war criminal, and had previously broadcast attacks on Hitler, Goering and the Nazis using Russian radio. He believed the German army had been sacrificed at Stalingrad. His appearance and presentation caused an uproar in the defendants' bench. He was cross-examined by nine defense lawyers. Although shaken, his evidence was clear.

Evidence was given regarding German orders requiring all Russian soldiers to be branded on the left buttock. They were to be poisoned if they were not fit for work. Official German records listed 130,000 prisoners of war tortured to death or shot at Maidanek. The evidence went on and on. A Russian film was shown depicting unbelievable atrocities too horrible to mention. It became clear the war in the east was prosecuted almost totally as an atrocity. After the film, the justices settled down and felt they could not interfere with the Russian case.

Even the defense counsel stopped cross-examining. Day after day the evidence piled on horror after horror. The evidence showed that Himmler's public statement that after the war only 30 million people would live in the east was in fact their aim. Survivors were to have no ties with the past, no science, no art, no religion. The war in the east was virtually a war of extermination.

At this time, Winston Churchill gave his famous speech at a university in Fulton, Missouri, in which he stated an iron curtain had descended across the continent. This gave the German defendants great solace and a feeling they were vindicated. The 73 days of the prosecution case ended on March 4, 1946. During the year there had been many other war crime trials, lynchings, and in France particularly, the shaving of heads of collaborators. At the beginning, most of the Germans assumed they would simply be found guilty and shot. However as the case proceeded, they began to hope because the judges seemed to be acting extremely fairly. Word circulated that the outcome was not preordained.

Although the defense wanted a three week delay before they started their case, the judges refused and forced the matter to continue uninterrupted. The defense was not well organized and in fact, rather than address many of the individual allegations, they elaborated on Germany's grievances with the Versailles Treaty that ended World War I.

One defense tactic used brilliantly by Doenitz's attorney was to request documents from the allies that showed their policies. For instance, Kranzbuehler obtained an order from the judges that he could send questions to Admiral Nimitz of the U.S. Navy in Hawaii asking questions about their policies dealing with submarine warfare. He did the same with the British admiralty. When the attorneys defending the diplomat Ribbentrop tried the same with the British foreign office, the records were declined, although they did agree they would answer some defense interrogatories (questions). As in any case, the defense had the ability to bring up issues that were very sensitive to the allies. The French treatment of German prisoners was an issue and had been the subject of an unfavorable Red Cross report. There were questions regarding the British violating the naval provisions of the Versailles Treaty. The defense specified that several governments including many of the allied powers had recognized the Nazi government in 1933. It forced the prosecution to put on evidence that recognition does not mean approval. There was an implication regarding Germany's invasion of Norway. There was evidence the British planned to do so, hence the Germans wanted to preempt that.

The case against Goering, since he was second only to Hitler, covered all four counts of the indictment. He was integral to the plan for aggressive war and played a major role in individual crimes such as the execution of captured airmen, the murder of 50 escaped but recaptured prisoners, and atrocities committed by the Hermann Goering Division. Goering personally was the genesis of the Gestapo and concentration camps while he was Prussian Minister of the Interior. He was in charge of the Four Year Plan which used slave labor. He stole thousands of pieces of art and most thought he was the most important defendant in the case. Being a leader, he had not only prepared an individual defense for himself but also for others on trial. However, many of Goering's witnesses were successfully attacked on cross-examination. His codefendants became worried but he tried to calm their fear by telling them to wait until he testified.

The justices made an important point of law at this juncture of the trial. The defendants tried to introduce evidence of allies' violation of international law but the Court upheld objections of Rudenko and Jackson who protested that violation by one side does not excuse the other.

On Wednesday, March 13, 1946, Goering took the stand. He was confident and made a good appearance. He had lost a lot of weight in captivity and being off drugs, his mind was clear. He was a relaxed witness and gave a statement which took two days. He described his involvement with pride, even bragging about his development of black markets in different countries. He completely accepted responsibility for the economic laws against Jews. Also, he was responsible for stripping the Russian economy. On the other hand, he did try and remove himself from individual atrocities including the burning of the Reichstag and concentration camp killings. He argued that the bombing of Poland included only military targets.

Upon cross-examination by other defense counsel, he threw life preservers out to many of the defendants. He was a master of the facts and testified in a persuasive manner. However, the bottom line was his admissions, amounted almost to guilt. His 12 hours of direct testimony were a remarkable display of his mental agility and physical strength.

When Justice Jackson started the cross-examination on March 18, 1946, he faced a pugnacious Goering. Rather than attack aggressively, Jackson wasted time dealing with early policies of the Nazis and how they took control of Germany. He jumped around and gave Goering opportunities to pontificate. Goering was quick to grasp the intent of almost every question and it was widely reported he "handled" Jackson. The Justice was particularly unhappy with the tribunal because they let Goering give speeches rather than answer questions. Realizing his freedom to pontificate, Goering gave even longer discourses and Jackson became more upset because the tribunal refused to force the witness to answer questions directly. In reality, the judges wanted to hear what Goering had to say. It was a humiliating experience for the U.S. Supreme Court Justice who did not recover. On too many occasions, Jackson used documents he was not familiar with and Goering explained they had no relevance to the question. On the third day, Jackson started to give speeches himself and he was obviously angry. Although he did obtain Justice Lawrence's agreement to ask the defendant to simply answer questions yes or no with short explanations, the Chief Justice was not firm and did not make the limits clear. Finally, Jackson gave up and the cross-examination was taken over by Maxwell-Fyfe. He asked very specific questions which were short, precise, and dealt with factual issues which could be used to impeach Goering, if Goering did not answer truthfully. He aggressively attacked Goering and obtained some inconsistent testimony. He managed to put the witness on the run. The following day the cross-examination was relentless and focused on the killing of the 50 British airmen who had escaped from Stalag Luft III. Goering had tried to evade responsibility by stating he was on leave but Maxwell Fyfe proved this was not the case.

Contemporary analysis of the handling of Goering concluded Justice Jackson lost control of his cross-examination because he lost control of himself thereby giving Goering an opportunity to score points and give speeches. Maxwell Fyfe's exact questioning and precise knowledge of the facts reversed the situation but left many believing Jackson had given the worst performance of the trial. In fairness, it was also agreed Justice Jackson gave the best opening statement and the best closing argument of any of the lawyers. However his reputation was sullied because of his handling of Goering's cross-examination.

The cases against the other defendants continued throughout the spring and summer of 1946. The defendants' summations began on August 31 and were not particularly interesting although some described Hitler as being cruel and having a tendency to madness. None of the defendants asked for mercy from the Court and they all appeared resigned to conviction. There was no admission of personal guilt in any of the defendants' statements. Those in the dock began blaming each other, several accusing Goering of failing to accept responsibility as the second head of state. The trial had taken 216 days and the justices adjourned to discuss judgment and verdicts. They held numerous meetings and agreed that a majority vote was required for a finding of guilty. Since the two judges from each country, actually one being the senior judge and the other the alternate, were required to vote in the same way it was agreed a 2 to 2 tie would not result in conviction. Chief Justice Lawrence announced the verdicts on October 1, 1946. Goering was convicted first, it being said, "His guilt is unique in its enormity" Hess was next followed by other justices announcing verdicts for the remaining defendants. That afternoon Schacht, Papen and Fritzscht were released to give a press conference. They all feared they might be brought before a German court. Some were amazed by the acquittal. Those found guilty were subsequently brought individually before the justices to hear their sentences. They were immediately handcuffed and led back to prison. Some, such as Albert Speer accepted the sentences as being reasonable. Hess had not listened and did not have any idea what his sentence was.

Requests for clemency were made and denied by the Allied Control Council on October 10, 1946. The 10 who were sentenced to death were hung in the Palace of Justice Gymnasium on the night of October 16, 1946. Goering escaped by committing suicide the day before. He had taken a cyanide capsule, which was thought to be secreted on his person since his arrest. Others thought his wife had given him the capsule during one of their visits. Others thought a guard had been bribed to give it to him.

What did the Nuremberg trial give us as precedent? Some thought it was the beginning of the enforcement of international law. Some thought the trial should have been held and overseen by the Germans.

Subsequently, the United Nations was invited to draft a code of international law which never occurred. Other conventions were agreed to such as the Protection of Human Rights and Basic Freedoms in

1950, and more recently the International Criminal Court at the Hague which the United States has refused to recognize.

There is much debate regarding the treatment of prisoners by officials of the United States. The test used revolves around the status of each prisoner. Status is determined by rules set forth in various Geneva Conventions. The most commonly recognized is prisoner of war (POW). Such an individual is often captured in battle and must fit the following criteria: wear a uniform and insignia recognizable at a distance; be a member of an organized military unit acting under a responsible commander; carry arms openly and conduct operations in accordance with the laws of war.

Perhaps the easiest individual to consider in applying this criteria would be a Taliban soldier or fighter. Their black robes and headdress could be construed as a uniform, they universally had long beards and were in recognized units of a national army, that of Afghanistan. If captured in uniform, they would be treated as POW's.

Those not fitting the criteria are not given the protections afforded POW's. For example, an enemy soldier in civilian clothing can be treated as a spy or saboteur and is subject to execution. In between a uniformed soldier and a spy or saboteur are many individuals at war against the United States, those that do not fight in uniform nor in organized and controlled units, and they have become known as unlawful or enemy combatants. Often these individuals are referred to as terrorists. These persons are not specifically protected by the Geneva Conventions since they do not fit the criteria of a prisoner of war. It is the lack of clarity regarding their status which has caused much concern. What are their rights, if any, under the U.S. constitution and the laws of the United States? The courts are presently dealing with these issues and no doubt results will address factors such as citizenship, geographical location and facts supporting the status of the person as decided by U.S. Government officials. Generally, U.S. law has not provided protections to foreign fighters or supporters of enemies of the United States who are not citizens of the United States and who are not specifically protected by U.S. law including treaties and conventions which when entered into by the United States are constitutionally made an important part of the U.S. law.

The military hearings taking place regarding each incarcerated individual's status must determine if the accused is a person who should be treated as a POW or should be appropriately held as an unlawful enemy combatant. Alternatively, it must be determined that the individual is neither and therefore should be released as many have been. Based on U.S. legal precedent, military tribunals, composition and operation is determined by the Executive Branch of the U.S. Government under its constitutional powers to conduct foreign policy and command the military. One of these treaties is Article 3 of the 1949 Geneva Conventions that require a "regularly constituted court affording all the judicial guarantees which are recognized as indispensable by civilized people" to carry out sentences or executions. In Hamdan v. Rumsfeld, the United States Supreme Court held Congress must provide for the makeup of such a court (miliary commissions or tribunals) and provide the fairness provisions it believes are indispensable specifically making them applicable to unlawful combatants even if they do not fit the definition of a POW. Also Hamdan held the defendant could not be tried for conspiracy to violate the laws of war. This follows the holding in Nuremburg that conspiracy alone is not a triable offense. Hence the U.S. Supreme Court has now found that "enemy combatants" who are not prisoners of war are in fact included in the Geneva Convention protections of the 1949 Treaties.

Questions exist about our concepts of fairness (such as speedier hearings) and the granting of our legal protections to non-citizens who are determined by the Executive Branch to be at war with the United States and who are not citizens or POW's. These unlawful combatants or terrorists have had basically no protections as we know them although they are gaining some based on our concepts of fairness and the decision in the Hamdan case. The most widely discussed is the protection from "torture." The Geneva Conventions against torture and our recently enacted laws deal with very specific definitions of torture. Basically, they preclude acts that result in permanent mental or physical injury. Many methods utilized by governments are definitely "cruel and unusual" as we think of that concept when considering our Constitutional protections but they do not result in permanent mental or physical injury. Sleep deprivation, the use of lights and sounds, uncomfortable and painful body positioning are examples.

It is the legal line between types of "torture" and the resulting damages that is properly in debate. History shows us that civilized nations have had to compromise their ideals based upon threat. To cross the line requires widespread acceptance of the danger which is often in opposition to the secrecy necessary to wage war when the battlefield is virtually everywhere. Should someone actually be captured who knows a "dirty bomb" will destroy a city in one hour, how far will the interrogators go to learn the location when failure means the death of family, friends and thousands of others? Would the threat and peril perceived cause one to cross the line? Would society accept the line being crossed? Human nature indicates the closer the line gets to our family and friends, the easier it will be to cross. We are not saints or sinners, just human. Most agree we are not yet at the line and hope we never reach it, but we should be preparing ourselves for the possible eventuality.

CHAPTER 10

STATE OF TEXAS V.
JACK RUBENSTEIN AKA JACK RUBY

JACK RUBY WAS BORN on April 11, 1911 in the Maxwell Street ghetto of Chicago making him 52 years of age at the time of the murder of Lee Harvey Oswald. His father was institutionalized for alcoholism when Ruby was a teenager. His mother had mental problems and could not care for him, consequently he ended up in a Jewish orphanage. Jack was well known to police officers around Wrigley Field because he was arrested on a number of occasions for scalping tickets. He was generally known to engage in petty crime. Moving to San Francisco in his 20's, Ruby became a distributor of the San Francisco Call Bulletin newspaper before moving on to Dallas in the late 1940's. Working at nightclubs, he learned the business and ultimately ended up owning striptease clubs. He lived with his sister in Dallas until the early 1960's when he obtained his own apartment. Ruby was familiar to Dallas police officers because of his ownership of nightclubs. In 1959, he went to Cuba to arrange for the sale of jeeps to Fidel Castro's government but the deal did not come to fruition.

At approximately 11:30 a.m. on November 24, 1963, after having snuck into the parking garage of the Dallas City Hall, which also served as police headquarters, he approached Lee Harvey Oswald who was in the custody of detectives and shot him in the stomach. He was quickly apprehended and disarmed. The entire incident was broadcast worldwide on television and most experts agreed virtually every person in the United States saw the crime committed on at least one occasion by viewing it on television or in movie theaters.

Immediately, many began to believe the Oswald killing was part of a conspiracy that included the assassination of John F. Kennedy two days before. In reviewing the event from the standpoint of prosecuting a murder, one again looks for motive, means and opportunity. There was no issue regarding the latter two. Obviously with the whole world literally watching, Ruby possessed the means and had gained the opportunity. But, mystery surrounded his motive and to this day conspiracy theorists still speak of Ruby being part of a huge plot to kill Oswald because Officer J.D. Tippit had failed to do so and was himself killed while pursuing Oswald shortly after the assassination of President Kennedy. Some theorists go further and state Ruby was the man in the grassy knoll who fired shots at Kennedy. Exhaustive investigation by the United States Secret Service, FBI, Dallas police, the Warren Commission, and Ruby's defense lawyers failed to develop any evidence Ruby was anything but emotional, unstable and very upset over the killing of John F. Kennedy who he considered a great person. Ruby made many statements shortly after his arrest which will be referred to in the following material and all of them indicate he simply saw an opportunity and acted on it. But, the handling of his case was not that simple.

During his trial, evidence was presented which proved he was at a Western Union telegraph office a short distance from City Hall until just a few minutes before the killing. He had gone there to wire money to a female dancer who had arrived to dance in his club the previous night, but Ruby had closed the club in honor of Kennedy. She told him she needed the cash, so he wired her $25 in Fort Worth. This evidence was presented not only by the woman but by the telegraph office operator. Four minutes after leaving the telegraph office he found himself in a crowd of reporters as Oswald was being ushered out of the police headquarters into the garage. While a police car was leaving, Ruby entered the garage by passing behind the open gate and the police officer stationed there. Suddenly he was confronted by Oswald and since it was his habit to carry a firearm (he had been arrested twice before for doing so), he pulled it out, approached Oswald and fired a shot. Testimony in the trial including statements made by Ruby to police officers lead one to believe he intended to fire at least three times but was precluded from doing so by a detective grabbing the revolver and covering the cylinder with his hand so that it would not turn before he jerked it from Ruby's grasp.

Information obtained in the investigation and included in the testimony during the trial showed the exact time Oswald left the jail could not possibly have been previously known by anyone. He was scheduled to depart at 10:00 a.m., and that had been advertised. Reporters had been hanging out and stayed well past 10:00 a.m., waiting for the event to occur. Delay was caused by the Dallas head of the Secret Service questioning Oswald and only when he completed his interrogation was Oswald escorted out of police headquarters into the garage. No one, not even the head of the Secret Service, would know beforehand when his questioning would have been completed and Ruby's being at a Western Union office until four minutes before the actual killing would indicate he was certainly not waiting around for an opportunity to murder Oswald who had delayed the departure a further 15 minutes by asking for a sweater.

Immediately after being arrested, Ruby was questioned by a number of detectives before his arraignment the following day. Statements made at the time of the murder and after he was arrested were entered into evidence albeit over objection. Initially, he was represented by an experienced Dallas criminal defense attorney named Tom Howard. This attorney immediately assessed the situation as being one wherein the best approach would be for Ruby to do a mea culpa and hope for a light sentence since, after all, the man he killed was despised and the shooting occurred in an emotional rage. However, Ruby's family and friends decided he needed a more experienced and better known attorney so they eventually ended up speaking with and hiring Melvin Belli of San Francisco, the most famous lawyer in California at that time and possibly in the United States. Known as the King of Torts, he had amassed an enviable record of verdicts in excess of $100,000 (a large amount at that time) over his years of practice and he was considered a brilliant orator. Initially, Belli asked for $75,000 up front as a fee but he finally agreed on $25,000 feeling he could make more money from "book rights." Arriving in Dallas with great fanfare, Belli immediately decided on a defense strategy which proposed not guilty by reason of insanity since Ruby suffered from psychomotor epilepsy and was supposedly in a seizure state at the time of the murder. Belli also, knowing he needed local presence, asked his old friend Joe Tonnahill, a well known Texas personal injury trial lawyer, to join the defense team. Needing a book lawyer, they hired former Deputy District Attorney Phil Burleson who had handled appellate matters for the Dallas County District Attorneys' Office. Tom Howard stayed on the team even though he questioned the intended defense strategy.

Texas law did not allow for the prosecution of a capital case to be initiated by a district attorney's "information". A grand jury was required to indict Ruby and did so. The defense team knew problems

Ruby faced included the facts that this crime was the most public crime in history, that the defendant was Jewish in an Anglo Saxon-Protestant community, that he owned a striptease nightclub, and that he had precluded authorities from getting information from Oswald regarding the assassination of John F. Kennedy. Most importantly he had humiliated Dallas police and the City of Dallas.

Feeling the best defense was a good offense, Belli decided they would try the victim who many thought should have been shot. Although attorney Howard did not think an insanity defense would sell, he did feel that showing mental instability would result in a light sentence. Howard thought they could prove the act was done without malice since in Texas if a person of "ordinary temperament" would have committed the murder it was presumed to have been without malice. He argued many people no doubt wanted to kill Oswald.

Melvin M. Belli was born in Sonora, California, on July 29, 1907. His father, Caesar, was a wealthy banker and investor who lost all his assets in the depression. Melvin put himself through the University of California's Boalt Hall Law School and graduated in 1933. Although smart enough for Law Review, he also liked to enjoy himself and he did not graduate high enough in his class to be hired by a large law firm. Being intelligent, imaginative, charming and hard working he had the combination of assets that were natural for a tort (personal injury) lawyer. Because he had developed a large amount of knowledge regarding medicine and was a pioneer in the use of demonstrative evidence in the courtroom, he enjoyed great success.

Belli used a blackboard and chalk to laboriously itemize and add up his client's damages. He was a practical joker, had a great sense of humor, and lived well beyond his means especially towards the end of his career. In his speeches and writings, he constantly fought the "Holy Grail Insurance Company." On the top of his building on Montgomery

Street in San Francisco, just west of Washington Street, he had a cannon that he fired and a skull and crossbones flag he flew to celebrate his victories.

Judge Joe Brown was not considered particularly bright but he was the assigning judge in his court at the time of Ruby's arraignment and knowing the case would generate much publicity, he decided to assign it to himself. Immediately he ordered that no television, radio or cameras would be allowed in the courtroom.

Leading the prosecution team was well known and experienced Dallas County District Attorney Henry Wade who had been a brilliant student at the University of Texas Law School, graduating magna cum laude in 1938. He spent four years with the FBI and left to join the Navy in 1943. Upon returning to Dallas after the war, he accepted a job as Assistant United States Attorney for a couple of years and then was elected Dallas County District Attorney, beginning service on January 1, 1951. He was considered able, honest and without political ambition. He became nationally known during his career because he was involved in a number of high profile cases including Roe v. Wade.

After Lee Harvey Oswald was arrested, Wade involved himself in the investigation, visiting police headquarters on numerous occasions in the next couple of days. He also gave press conferences and discussed evidence, which he should not have done. Backing up Wade was Bill Alexander, a notorious Dallas prosecutor known as the "Hatchet Man" of the District Attorney's office. He had been involved in just about every major Dallas felony trial for 15 years and although not particularly liked, he was well respected. The third member of the team, Jim Bowie, was Henry Wade's chief assistant and considered to be the book man on the prosecution team.

As mentioned, Belli disagreed with Howard's strategy as "begging for mercy." Belli wanted to use his medical knowledge and obtain a verdict of not guilty by reason of diminished capacity amounting to insanity. The defense moved to release Ruby on bail and for a change of venue. After putting on evidence of Ruby's distress about the killing of John F. Kennedy plus some medical testimony, the defense dropped their motion for change of venue when the Judge indicated he probably would not grant it, but they did convince the Judge to take the other motion under submission. Although the prosecution initially opposed the bail motion, they realized they were getting a free look at the defense case so they sat back, listened, and obtained plenty of advance information from which to prepare their case and counter the defense. After a Christmas 1963 recess, the hearing was not reconvened. The Judge did not appear to agree the killing was a result of an inflamed agitated mind and therefore not premeditated. The Judge felt there was no reason to allow bail. Texas law precluded bail if the evidence was clear the defendant committed a capital offense with malice.

Texas followed the M'Naghten rule regarding insanity. M'Naghten was a wood worker from Glasgow, Scotland. He had worked for his father as an apprentice and journeyman but when his father refused to make him a partner he left and ended up in London in July, 1842. Six months later he shot and killed Edward Drummond, the private secretary to Prime Minister Richard Robert Peel. Apparently M'Naghten had mistaken Drummond for Sir Robert. He was tried for murder on March 3 and 4, 1843 at the Central Criminal Court in London. During his trial, evidence showed he frequently complained of head pains, had exhibited episodes of over excitement, walked in his sleep, broke into fits of laughter and frequently talked incoherently. The medical testimony was unanimous that although he appeared reasonably normal, M'Naghten had a disease of the mind which precluded him from controlling himself against passions and impulses that in this case compelled him to kill. The doctors testified M'Naghten suffered from delusions that resulted in the killing of Drummond.

He was acquitted by the jury but was incarcerated in a hospital for 20 years before dying. The acquittal outraged many in England, and the House of Lords asked the Judges of England to review the law on this subject. The result was known as the M'Naghten rule: The accused was not criminally responsible if he was laboring "under such a defect of reason from a disease of the mind, as not to know the nature and quality of the act he was doing, or if he did know it, that he did not know that he was doing what was wrong." Simply put, could the perpetrator know right from wrong at the time of the act? Leopold and Loeb could not utilize this defense because they obviously knew right from wrong.

Although Texas followed the M'Naghten rule, it put the burden on the defense to prove the defendant so suffered by a preponderance (something is more probable than not) of the evidence. This is the rule followed by approximately half the states. The other half require proof beyond a reasonable doubt. It is well known lawyers like the rule and psychiatrists do not since there are so many nuances involved in determining if a person knows an act is right or wrong. The public often believes the defense of insanity is a lawyer's trick and hence the defense has a difficult burden to prove the argument is not a sham. Since many probably wanted to kill Oswald, Tom Howard thought it would be difficult to prove that a person who actually did so was insane. On February 14, 1964, Judge Brown finally ruled on the motion for a change of venue and denied it. His position was they should try and get a jury and the prosecution agreed.

On March 3, 1964, a jury was selected. Texas law did not provide for alternates. 162 jurors had been examined and were considered a smart group since the members had above-average educations. Judge Brown denied all initial motions and then heard further motions. These motions included issues dealing with the defense wanting two more jury peremptory challenges and an issue regarding the right to a public trial since the court's public relations officer had assigned just about all of the seats to members of the press to the exclusion of the general public. Belli wanted Ruby's two sisters to be present since they were his only family, but the Judge had excluded all potential witnesses. Belli also made motions raising the issue of Ruby's sanity and competence to stand trial. (This issue was also dealt with in the case of The United States v. Ezra Pound.) Although Texas law allowed for a separate trial on the competency issue, it is thought the defense really did not want such a trial and simply wanted to raise the issue so they could create another avenue of appeal. In fact, the motion was untimely in that it was brought quite late.

Now that the trial had started and a jury was present, the defense attorneys began acting much more professionally and avoided foolish motions. When police officers were called by the prosecution Belli, on cross-examination, showed they knew Ruby as being emotional and excitable before the JFK assassination. After the murder of JFK, Ruby tried to get close to Oswald by hanging around police headquarters. He volunteered to get sandwiches for the interrogating detectives, he helped the press identify police officers, the sheriff and other officials. He hung out with the reporters and in fact some reporters resented it. All this took place on the day before he killed Oswald.

Detective James R. Leavelle, to whom Oswald was handcuffed, testified regarding events at the time of the shooting. Most of the issues dealt with statements allegedly made by Ruby. One must distinguish between statements made by the defendant before he was arrested and those after. Statements made by the defendant after he was in custody would normally not be admissible unless they were classified as "res gestae" exclamations made not as a result of questioning.

A number of police officers testified that as Ruby approached Oswald with his gun out, he stated, "you son of a bitch." This evidence was presented by the prosecution. On the other hand, the defense produced reporters and a radio announcer with a microphone who was right in front of Oswald and none of them heard that alleged statement nor was it picked up by the microphone.

After he was taken into custody a number of detectives testified Ruby made the following statements:

1. "I hope I killed the son of a bitch"
2. "I did it because you couldn't do it"
3. "I intended to get all three shots"
4. "I did it to show the world that Jews have guts"
5. "I did it so Jackie Kennedy would not have to come to Dallas to trial"
6. "I first thought of killing him at the Friday night press conference"

There was corroboration of the first five statements beyond the testimony of the police officer. However, the sixth and most damaging statement, because it indicated premeditation, could not be corroborated and the only testimony regarding that assertion made was by Sergeant Patrick T. Dean. Allegedly it was made in the presence of Senior Secret Service Agent Sorrels but he could not remember the remark.

At the close of the prosecution, Belli made the usual motion for a directed verdict of acquittal which was summarily denied. He then proceeded with an opening statement which stated the defendant acted at a time when he suffered from a seizure caused by psychomotor epilepsy, and did not appreciate or know what he was doing. District Attorney Wade had been concerned regarding Belli's reputation as a great orator and had anxiously awaited his opening statement, but there was nothing particularly astounding about the speech and the prosecution relaxed.

Belli called the singer, Little Lynn, and the Western Union telegraph operator who had a date and time stamped copy of the message to show Ruby was at a different location just a few minutes before the shooting.

He called a witness named William Serur who testified regarding Ruby's unusual relationship with his dogs. Apparently Ruby constantly referred to his dogs as his children and allowed them to demolish his living quarters and car. This seemed strange to Serur who Ruby asked to provide a car repair estimate, and he further testified regarding Ruby's unusual comments regarding his "children." Mrs. Patricia Kohs was called to testify she witnessed Jack Ruby push a cab driver down a staircase and immediately after say, "Did I do that?" This was an attempt to show that Ruby had, on a prior occasion, acted aggressively and did not realize or remember that he actually did so. Unfortunately, Belli impeached his own witness because he brought out the fact that she had been arrested for drug use which was something the prosecution would not have been able to develop since they were only misdemeanor arrests.

Belli called Ike Pappas of WNEW, a New York radio broadcaster, who testified he was right in front of Oswald with his mike and it did not pick up Ruby's alleged statement as he approached Oswald. Other reporters also testified on this point.

Thereafter, the defense opened the "battle of the experts." Defense experts had to prove insanity by a preponderance of the evidence before a jury who were no doubt sitting there saying to themselves, which experts do we believe? Belli's first witness was Dr. Ray Schafer of Yale University, a clinical psychologist. He testified the difference between psychiatry and psychology was that the former concentrates on the diagnosis and treatment of medical disorders while the latter overlaps psychiatry and further tests, studies, and treats human behavior. Lacking medical training psychologists are less concerned about physical treatment. His diagnosis after examination of Ruby and reviewing the results of ten tests was that he had organic brain damage specifically psychomotor epilepsy. He had an IQ of 109 which was higher than 73 percent of the American male population at that time.

The prosecution strenuously objected to Dr. Schafer's testimony since he would not testify regarding the defendant's ability to tell right from wrong. Initially, Judge Brown sustained the objection and excluded Dr. Schafer's testimony. Belli was incredulous and of course argued that Dr. Schafer's testimony was a foundation for later testimony by other experts, i.e., a psychiatrist who would state Ruby could not appreciate the difference between right and wrong at the time of the act. When Judge Brown appeared to continue to sustain the objection, the prosecution team became concerned because they realized Belli was absolutely correct and that if Judge Brown excluded this testimony it would be good grounds for appeal and probably reversal of a guilty verdict. The prosecutors started backtracking and finally Henry Wade advised the Judge to "let's let him go on...." At that point the Judge changed his ruling and allowed the testimony. Unfortunately, although Belli won the battle it moved him off his stride to the extent that the balance of his examination of Dr. Schafer was quite poor. Of course, Judge Brown excluding this evidence would have been in error in all 50 states of the United States. A party is allowed to present foundation evidence which other witnesses can relate to the actual question at issue and Judge Brown seemingly forgot that basic rule.

On the other hand, Henry Wade was not experienced in the cross-examination of medical witnesses, therefore he did not take on Dr. Schafer regarding the specifics of his tests, but he did establish from this witness that, based upon his knowledge, Ruby did not seem confused nor was he in a fugue state at the time of the shooting of Oswald. This is important because psychomotor epilepsy puts a person in a state of seizure, a fugue state, a state of consciousness in which one could not know what they were doing and normally would not remember it.

Belli next called Dr. Martin Dowler, an expert in electroencepholograms. He testified he took a history from Ruby and this was the first time evidence was admitted regarding Ruby's background. Although the prosecution objected to the history being given as self serving, the Judge overruled the objection and was correct in doing so. The objection was based on hearsay, however evidence admitted for any proper purpose can be admitted even though it may be inadmissible for other reasons.

Dr. Dowler testified Ruby suffered from a seizure disorder brought about by frequent fights involving head injuries. During a seizure the person does not know right from wrong, he is an automaton. But, he also stated many times that the person would not remember events that occurred during such a seizure and the prosecution had the police testimony regarding Ruby's statements immediately after the shooting. On cross-examination, Wade obtained an admission from the doctor that he, in fact, did not know if Ruby was or was not in a seizure state at the time of the shooting.

Belli next called Manfried S. Guttmacher, M.D., of Harvard University, a psychiatrist. He testified Ruby told him he shot Oswald on a momentary sudden impulse. Unfortunately for the defense, the witness did not mention psychomotor epilepsy. After the trial Belli stated Dr. Guttmacher had advised him on the eve of the trial, March 3, 1964, that he thought Belli's psychomotor epilepsy medical theory was medically unsound and legally imprudent.

In effect, Belli was faced with one of his main expert witnesses not agreeing with his theory of the case and in fact espousing the theory of "sudden impulse" which at that time was gaining some notoriety.

Unfortunately, Belli had not predicated the defense on the theory of "sudden impulse" and could not change horses mid-stride. Reviewing the case as a whole, the result probably would not have been any different.

During cross-examination of Dr. Guttmacher, prosecutor Bill Alexander went into the facts of the shooting to prove Ruby was not in a fugue or seizure state. When taking a history Dr. Guttmacher had asked Ruby why he had not shot more than once and his response was "I didn't shoot more than once because they grabbed my hand." Interestingly, he obtained this witness' expert testimony that Ruby, in this doctor's opinion, was not in a psychomotor epileptic seizure state at the time of the shooting. In effect he used this expert to disprove the defense theory and he should have ended his examination with that startling admission. Unfortunately, Alexander did what many lawyers unhappily do and that is he tried to "gild the Lilly" and hammer home a point. Experience has shown that when a lawyer on cross-examination does this, most of the time the witness waters down the admission and the lawyer regrets having not stopped while ahead. In fact, any lawyer can have a transcript of the testimony prepared and the quote can later be argued to the jury. Hence, once you get the right words out of a witness mouth it is always better to stop. In this case, given the second opportunity, Guttmacher weakened his prior admission by adding that Ruby may have been in a fugue state resulting from a seizure and that he, the witness, felt it was an event of episodic dyscentral, i.e., temporary insanity. The net result was the witness agreed Ruby was temporarily insane but did not agree the cause was psychomotor epilepsy seizure as testified to by the other experts and as espoused by Belli.

Belli did not put Ruby on the stand because he was concerned the defendant would boast about the crime and why he did it, i.e., for "Jackie and the children" as he had suggested to Sergeant Patrick Dean shortly after the murder. Dr. Guttmacher told Belli that was a realistic risk and advised against putting Ruby on as a witness. Therefore, Belli rested the defense case.

The prosecution's rebuttal witnesses included the other two doctors on the panel, Stubberfield and Holbrook, who examined Ruby at the request of the Court. However, first they called a young neurologist named Olinger, not very experienced, who testified he disagreed with the defense witnesses regarding the EEG results. He did not feel they showed psychomotor epilepsy. Dr. Stubblefield testified that based on his examination and Ruby's statements that Ruby knew right from wrong at the time of the shooting. Dr. Holbrook testified he disagreed with psychologist Schafer, stating that he saw Ruby before Schafer and at that time Ruby had not developed the symptoms described by Schafer.

After some minor rebuttal and surrebuttal, the case was given to the jury which found, in two hours and 20 minutes, the defendant guilty of premeditated murder with malice and sentenced him to death. Belli lambasted Dallas and its injustice and shortly thereafter was fired.

After the trial, Ruby's friends and family tried to get him other representation and for a short time famed Texas criminal law attorney Percy Foreman and constitutional rights attorney William Kundsler acted on Ruby's behalf. Judge Brown eventually recused himself since he was writing a book regarding the trial and while the matter was on appeal, Ruby died of cancer.

The trial did not satisfactorily answer the question why? Ruby told the Warren Commission he killed Oswald so Jackie would not have to testify. There was a lot of stress in the United States at that time and apparently Ruby, given the means and opportunity, suddenly acted on it, alone. Ruby's death did nothing to settle the conspiracy theory that still follows the assassination of President John F. Kennedy but it is most probable Ruby did not shoot Oswald as part of such a plan.

CHAPTER 11

United States of America v. David t. Dellinger, Rennard C. Davis, Thomas E. Hayden, Abbott H. Hoffman, Jerry C. Rubin, Lee Weiner And John R. Froines Aka "The Chicago Seven"

THE ATMOSPHERE IN THE United States during 1968 was charged. The anti-Vietnam war movement was gaining momentum, General Westmoreland had requested over 200,000 additional troops, President Johnson had announced he would not seek re-election, Martin Luther King had been assassinated in April, and Robert F. Kennedy in June. In late January 1968 during the celebration of the Tet holiday, the North Vietnamese and Viet Cong launched an offensive sufficient to convince President Johnson to begin negotiations in Paris. In March, the My-Lai Massacre had occurred and General Creyton Abrams replaced General Westmoreland. The Kent State incident had not yet occurred and mass demonstrations at universities, in various cities and in Washington D.C. had not yet taken place. The country was on edge and while the hippie movement was developing in San Francisco, the defendants in Chicago were calling Judge Julius Hoffman the country's "Top Yippie".

Beginning on or about August 12, 1968 and continuing through August 30, 1968, the defendants allegedly gave various speeches in New York and Chicago requesting individuals assemble in Chicago during the Democratic National Convention to demonstrate against the war in Vietnam. Failing to obtain a permit for parades and demonstrations, the organizers nevertheless requested assemblies of persons to march to the International Amphitheatre, Lincoln Park, the Conrad Hilton Hotel and various areas surrounding these locations. During these events, the defendants were alleged to have given speeches to these assemblages requesting they "hold the park" against police efforts to clear it. They also allegedly made weapons and suggested objects be thrown at police and National Guard troops. They were also supposed to have obstructed traffic, damaged and seized property. The Government argued the defendants' actions violated various sections of Title 18 of the United States Code which makes it unlawful to incite, organize, promote, encourage or participate in a riot, commit acts of violence in furtherance of a riot, or aid and abet others to do so. The statute also makes it unlawful to teach and demonstrate to other persons the use, application and manufacture of incendiary devices, intending that said devices would be unlawfully employed for use in and in furtherance of civil disorders. Finally, they were charged with obstructing, impeding and interfering with firemen and law enforcement officers lawfully engaged in the performance of their official duties incident to and during the commission of civil disorders in violation of sections of Title 18. The Government also claimed David T. Dellinger, Rennard C. Davis and Thomas E. Hayden maintained an office in Chicago for the National Mobilization Committee to end the War in Vietnam and using that organization, they planned and organized the activities which took place in Chicago with the aid of the others indicted and numerous unindicted co-conspirators.

The trial of the Chicago Seven began before Judge Julius Hoffman on September 24, 1969, in the United States District Court for the Northern District of Illinois, Eastern Division, in the Federal Building in Chicago, Illinois. Defendants' lead attorneys were William Kunstler and Leonard Weinglass. The United States was represented by deputy attorney generals Richard Schultz and Thomas Foran. The trial lasted 4 1/2 months from September 24, 1969 until February 7, 1970 and is generally considered the most rancorous courtroom event in the judicial history of the United States. Constant interruptions by individual defendants, the disrespectful attitude of the defense lawyers and the partisanship of those attending the trial resulted in an unprecedented and yet to be surpassed series of contempt citations too numerous to individually consider. Defendant Abbie Hoffman, alone, was found guilty of 24 specifications of contempt and received sentences ranging from one day to two months for each individual count. Defense attorney Kunstler was personally found guilty of 24 separate occasions of contemptible conduct and received individual sentences of from 14 days to three months on each charge. His total sentence exceeded four years. The other defendants also were cited for contempt on numerous occasions; however, none of the defendants actually served any time for their contemptible conduct. Upon being found guilty of some substantive counts in the indictment, their contempt sentences were allowed to be served concurrently with the five year sentences imposed for the criminal convictions which were subsequently reversed.

The Grand Jury brought the indictment in September 1968. Bobby Seale was included as the eighth individual actually indicted; however, his case was severed from the other seven during the trial. Because he was so disruptive, the judge sent him to prison immediately for contempt.

18 other individuals were named in the indictment as conspirators but were not themselves indicted. Count I of the indictment alleged all of those indicted took part in conspiracies to commit various overt acts; however, subsequent counts also alleged individual actions on the part of each defendant in violation of other specific sections of Title 18 of the United States Code. The jury found each defendant guilty on the individual action counts and not guilty of the conspiracy allegations.

Since Count I alleged, among other overt acts, numerous instances of speeches by individual defendants as well as conduct, the jury no doubt decided it did not want to deal with the various First Amendment freedom of speech defenses argued by the defendants. They apparently felt more comfortable finding the defendants guilty of specific conduct in furtherance of the riots and these violations generally carried a penalty of five years imprisonment.

The defendants were radical on the issue of Vietnam. They had issues with the American judicial system, specifically, how it treated criminals. They also decried the treatment of blacks in the United States. Although some attempts were made during the trial to give the illusion the defendants were boys, by referring to them using youthful sounding names such as Abbie, Tom and Jerry, the reality was they were all mature, highly educated, men who knew exactly what they wanted and what they were doing. About the trial, Abbie Hoffman stated, "It's going to be a combination Scopes trial, revolution in the streets, Woodstock Festival and Peoples' Park, all rolled into one." Jay Miller of the American Civil Liberties Union stated, "It's going to be the most important political trial in the history of the United States."

Mayor Richard Daley told the Press: "Gentlemen, let's get something straight. The police aren't in the streets to create disorder, they are in the streets to preserve (the right to) disorder." That statement takes a little thought as to the Mayor's exact meaning, but he was obviously and artfully pointing out the police were there also to preserve rights to lawfully demonstrate. After the trial, a juror stated, "Would you like your children to grow up like them?"

The prosecution called many witnesses, including over 30 police officers, to testify regarding specific events. William Kunstler, in his summation, pointed out most of the officers did not appear in uniform. He alleged that was an attempt by the prosecution to avoid the appearance of a police state. Some of the police officer witnesses were undercover officers who attended various rallies, speeches, etc. One witness, Dwayne Oklepek, was a reporter who also attended a number of meetings and events. Factually, there was little question about many of the main points the prosecution wanted to prove. There was, in fact, a riot, the defendants were definitely participants in the events and the demonstrations did get out of control. Although the defendants tried to blame the police for the loss of control, the jury did not accept that argument. The actions of the defendants and their demeanor during the trial and in some legal minds, the demeanor and statements of the defense attorneys, almost insured the defendants would be found guilty.

A reading of the trial transcript reveals Judge Julius Hoffman to be patient and thorough. The defendants approached the trial as the beginning of a revolution. Abbie Hoffman told Judge Hoffman that he [the Judge] was creating millions of revolutionaries. He told the Judge that he had done more to destroy the court system in this country than any of the defendants could have done. He pointed out all they did was go to Chicago and the police system exposed itself as totalitarian. Abbie Hoffman used a quote from Abraham Lincoln's 1861 First Inaugural Address which stands the test of time and which should be remembered. "When the people shall grow weary of their constitutional right to amend the government, they shall exert their revolutionary right to dismember and overthrow that government."

The final chapter in this epic was the reversal of all the convictions by the Federal Court of Appeals. It found Judge Hoffman interfered with the defendants' rights to obtain an unbiased jury by refusing to allow defense counsels' questions, and the contempt convictions were overturned because they all exceeded six months, hence the law required the defendants be given the right to a jury trial which had not been provided.

The government, not wanting to continue the legal warfare, did not pursue a new trial. Judges were left to ponder how to control unruly defendants (and occasionally their lawyers) and those with a mind to be disruptive during trial have a blueprint for doing so. Saddam Hussein took points from this trial and followed the disruptive precedents in his trial. His defense counsel, former U.S. Attorney General Ramsey Clark, was certainly knowledgeable of the Chicago Seven case.

Chapter 12

United States v. Daniel Ellsberg

DANIEL ELLSBERG WAS RAISED in Detroit, Michigan and obtained a Ph.D. in economics from Harvard University. He was familiar with the military, having been a Marine Corps officer who rose to the rank of First Lieutenant. He served as a Company Commander during part of his two years of active service. Dr. Ellsberg became employed as an analyst by the Rand Corporation and accepted a position at the Pentagon as an assistant to John T. McNaughton, Assistant Secretary of Defense for International Security Affairs who reported directly to Secretary of Defense Robert McNamara. Later he served as a civilian employee of the State Department in Vietnam and became convinced the United States could not prevail in war against North Vietnam. As the war escalated in the late 60's, Ellsberg became disaffected and having access to secret documents known as the "Pentagon Papers" he attempted to have their contents published. The voluminous documents covered the period 1945 through 1965, and dealt with United States' relations and activities with regard to Vietnam. Daniel Ellsberg believed they reflected United States governmental action inconsistent with our values and with publicly stated positions. Attempting to have some of the information disclosed on the floor of Congress, he sought to have public debate surrounding the contents of the documents. Since no member of Congress would provide information from these documents on the floor of Congress, where they were immune from prosecution, he decided to turn the material over to Neil Sheehan, a New York Times reporter with whom he had become acquainted in Saigon. Ellsberg felt that if the facts became known it would change public perception regarding the war and result in the United States withdrawing from the conflict. Some would argue disclosing the information and the resulting public outcry actually aided and abetted the North Vietnamese. Peace negotiations were taking place during 1970 and 1971 and the more the United States' public became upset, the more entrenched North Vietnamese negotiators became in their positions. Many in the administration presumed the publication caused numerous lives to be lost because of the continuation of war. The last United States ground combat forces left Vietnam in August 1972. The air war continued and finally all American personnel left Vietnam at the end of April 1975.

There is substantial historical evidence indicating there was a good opportunity for a cease fire in Vietnam as the Johnson administration came to an end in 1968. Robert McNamara resigned as Secretary of Defense and negotiations were taking place in Paris. President Nixon took office and he introduced the concept of "Vietnamization" of the war. During 1969, the Third Marine Division was withdrawn, followed shortly by elements of the 82nd Airborne Division. In late 1969, the My Lai massacre became known and the war continued to divide the nation. In March 1969, Defense Secretary Laird stated U.S. forces would be withdrawn in substantial numbers. In November 1969, Nixon addressed the nation on television, appealed for national unity, and announced he would be pulling U.S. troops out of Vietnam in an orderly scheduled timetable. In December 1969, Ambassador Lodge resigned as the head U.S. negotiator in Paris due to a deadlock in the peace talks.

In response to the stalemate, Nixon expanded the war and initiated the bombing of Cambodia. As 1970 progressed both sides limited their ground warfare engagement and U.S. soldiers had been reduced to approximately 330,000. The casualty rate had been cut in half and the last major ground operation took place in September 1970. Vietnamization continued and the Vietcong initiated a guerrilla campaign to destroy the Vietnamization program. In May 1970, four students at Kent State were shot by the National Guard during a protest over the invasion of Cambodia. In June, a new North Vietnamese Army and Vietcong offensive began in Cambodia and all U.S. combat troops were withdrawn from Cambodia. The United States continued massive B-52 strikes along the DMZ in the summer of 1970. The war in Laos and Cambodia then escalated in 1971 and South Vietnamese troops entered Laos and Cambodia with U.S. air support. U.S. troop levels in Vietnam fell from 280,000 to 157,000 during 1971. In May huge protests took place in Washington D.C., and in June the New York Times serialized the "Pentagon Papers."

The U.S. government took action to halt publication of the documents and Daniel Ellsberg was arrested. The Supreme Court of the United States acted quickly and quashed the government's attempt to suppress publication of the papers. Reductions of U.S. forces in Vietnam continued throughout 1971 and into 1972. The South Vietnamese Army known as the ARVN took over the ground fighting, and the United States mined Hai-Phong harbor in May to strike at Hanoi's supply lines. Also, Nixon offered a complete withdrawal of troops in return for a cease fire and release of POWs. In June, Hanoi publicly stated the mining was causing severe economic problems and in July the Paris peace talks resumed.

The war continued until April 1975 when the South Vietnamese Army was defeated and the North Vietnamese offensive came to Saigon. The last U.S. embassy personnel left on April 28, 1975. On April 30, 1975 the South Vietnamese surrendered. Did the publication of the Pentagon Papers speed up the U.S. withdrawal of forces that had been announced prior to the release of the documents? The answer is probably yes. Would the war have ended sooner thus saving lives had the Pentagon Papers not been published, probably not. There was never any indication the North Vietnamese would accept anything but complete surrender and control of South Vietnam since their objective was total reunification.

After release of the top secret Defense Department history of the United States' role in Southeast Asia, Ellsberg was arrested and charged with a section of the espionage laws dealing with disclosure of secrets. The extent to which the administration of President Nixon responded to Ellsberg's acts was not known for a couple of years, but it was because of the "leaks" of the Pentagon Papers that the "Plumbers" group was established and they were to play an important part in the ultimate disposition of United States v. Ellsberg, as well as the resignation of President Nixon.

Immediately after the documents were leaked, the FBI's Domestic Intelligence Division zeroed in on Ellsberg and recommended that FBI Director Hoover permit New York agents to interview Ellberg's father-in-law millionaire toy manufacturer Lewis Marx. However, Hoover and Marx were acquaintances and, at Christmas time, Ellsberg's father-in-law often sent Hoover a large shipment of free toys to be distributed to the children of friends and to Hoover's favorite charities. Hoover refused to authorize the interview, but agents had already visited with Marx who reportedly did not particularly admire Ellsberg. Nixon's aides, upon hearing of Hoover's refusal, became furious and ordered a parallel investigation. E. Howard Hunt, Jr., recently appointed the "chief plumber", along with Nixon and his aides, decided it would be important to obtain information regarding Ellsberg and his alleged unusual lifestyle. When the defendant's former psychoanalyst, Dr. Lewis Fielding of Beverly Hills, refused to be interviewed by the FBI (properly so because of ethical guidelines), the White House asked the CIA for a psychiatric profile of Ellsberg to be drawn from public sources and the limited information contained in government files. The CIA paper concluded that although Ellsberg was probably passing through a midlife crisis and found himself "not nearly having achieved the prominence and success he expected and desired," he in fact "seemed to be responding to what he deemed a higher order of patriotism" and "saw himself as having a special mission."

The White House, not satisfied and believing Ellsberg had political and emotional motivations, wanted to identify any accomplices from his psychoanalyst's files. Therefore Hunt and G. Gordon Liddy, former FBI agents, went to Los Angeles in August 1971 to determine the feasibility of surreptitiously entering Fielding's office. Finding it would not be difficult, they returned on September 3, 1971, accompanied by a team of Cuban exiles from Miami opposed to Fidel Castro and willing to do anything in the cause against Communism. Burglarizing Fielding's office, they found nothing of importance.

Shortly after the initial publication and the Supreme Court's refusal to quash the newspaper's printing the story on the basis of the First Amendment, Ellsberg and his associate, Anthony J. Russo, Jr., were indicted under the Espionage Act and charged with receiving stolen property. The indictment proceedings took quite a while before they were actually concluded and six months more passed before jury selection started in June 1972 before Judge Byrne. The Judge, a former federal prosecutor, was determined to doggedly move the trial forward. Jury selection became a lengthy process because, at that time, many military related industries were located in southern California. Finally, a jury was impaneled in late July and opening statements were about to begin when the government "disclosed an interception" as a result of a wire tap in a national security related matter which contained a conversation by one of the defendants and his lawyers and consultants. Judge Byrne refused to halt the trial or hold a special hearing on the issue. The Ninth U.S. Circuit Court of Appeals agreed but Justice William O. Douglas, on vacation in Washington state, had jurisdiction over emergency appeals in the Ninth Circuit and agreed to hear arguments in a courtroom in Yakima, Washington. After the hearing, Douglas decided to stop the trial until the full Supreme Court could rule. However, the high court refused to convene a special session and Byrne had to excuse the jury until October. The Supreme Court did not address the matter until after Nixon was re-elected in November 1972 and Byrne, accepting a warning from the Ninth Circuit that it would be foolish to proceed with the same jury, no doubt tainted by publicity in the case, agreed to dismiss the matter and start over.

Trial again started on January 17, 1973 and the second jury was selected much more expeditiously. At the time, the Watergate burglars themselves were on trial in Washington. The Ellsberg trial droned on and became a battle of experts over whether or not the disclosure of the papers constituted a threat to national security. Because of other major issues in the news, such as negotiations to end the war and the release of American prisoners of war, the trial itself did not obtain much publicity.

On April 26, 1973, the Watergate prosecutors in Washington, having just learned of the "Plumber's" burglary of Dr. Field's office, notified Judge Byrne of the constitutional violation and governmental misconduct. Initially, Judge Byrne did not believe the action affected the evidence but, shortly after that, it was learned Ellsberg himself had been overheard in wire taps and that the logs were missing. Judge Byrne became frustrated over the government's misconduct, and dismissed the charges on May 11, 1973. Therefore, the issues before the court were never decided.

Interestingly, shortly after the dismissal, the *Washington Star-News* reported that Judge Byrne had visited the Nixon White House at San Clemente to discuss the possibility of becoming FBI director, suggesting the administration had been trying to have influence over Byrne's decisions. It was well known Judge Byrne had higher aspirations but his actions probably were a cause of his staying a U.S. District Court Judge which is an enviable position in and of itself.

Ellsberg and Russo were never actually acquitted of the charges against them. On July 12, 1974, Nixon's aide Erlichman, Liddy and the Cubans were found guilty of conspiracy to violate Dr. Fielding's civil rights, Liddy pleaded guilty to obstructing justice and in August 1974, Nixon resigned. Ellsberg's friend Russo did serve time in jail for his refusal to testify before the Los Angeles Federal Grand Jury. Ellsberg himself was not incarcerated.

There is no direct evidence the publication of the Pentagon Papers (thousands of documents), which were actually not read by very many people including members of Congress, actually helped end the war sooner. The U.S. Supreme Court decision in the cases of New York Times v. United States and United States v. Washington Post resulted in the six justices in the majority (three in the minority) finding that the Justice Department had not sustained its heavy burden of proof in order to obtain a prior restraint of the publication and the individual justices lambasted both the press and the government in their opinions. In fact, the Supreme Court decision can be used to obtain the prior restraint of information since it sets forth the principle that such can result if the applicant can sustain a heavy burden of proof. Since the decision stated it was possible, a publication can be restrained while the issues are under consideration by the court. The press was not particularly pleased with this result.

Considering events that took place in Iraq, Afghanistan and the United States, as a result of publication of prisoner abuse, and the Iraq war itself, some can again turn attention to whether or not the publication of controversial material during a time of war is beneficial to the pursuit of the war and/or a faster termination of hostilities. Considering the seriousness of war, one might think long and hard about politicizing it, thereby turning a deadly endeavor into a battle of talking heads on television. On the other hand, we should not go to war unless absolutely necessary and the public generally accepts the obligations that result. The invasions of Iraq and Afghanistan have not been accepted as necessary by a large number of Americans. Democracy in Iraq and Afghanistan, if such be the result, will be welcome but many Iraqis and others in the Middle East have distrust in democracy and express that distrust with violence.

CHAPTER 13

JERRY FALWELL V. HUSTLER MAGAZINE AND LARRY C. FLYNT

HUSTLER MAGAZINE, OWNED AND operated by Larry Flynt, published what it claimed to be a parody making fun of Jerry Falwell, leader of the religious right, using a Compari ad format. An ad campaign was published in numerous magazines wherein Compari used entertainment and other personalities to make statements regarding the first time they drank that beverage. Using this format, Hustler Magazine printed copy that referred to Falwell's first time having sex. The ad was obviously mean spirited and outrageous since it used Falwell's mother as the object of his initial sexual encounter and placed the occurrence in an outhouse.

The trial took place in the federal courtroom of Judge James C. Turk in Roanoke, Virginia, a venue quite familiar to Jerry Falwell. Although it was held in 1983, final decision was not rendered until February 24, 1988. Previously Falwell had brought suit against Penthouse Magazine which published an article by two independent writers who had interviewed Falwell. There being no agreement as to where the article would be published and there being no issue that the contents were false because the interview had been given, the Court found against Falwell and in favor of Penthouse. Normon Ray Grutman was Penthouse's attorney in that case and he treated Falwell very aggressively. When Falwell decided to bring the action against Hustler he hired Grutman, notwithstanding his Jewish religion, hoping he would treat Larry Flynt just as aggressively and prevail.

Falwell's complaint alleged the publication by Hustler appropriated Falwell's name and likeness for the purpose of advertisement or trade, without his consent. The second cause of action was for libel, alleging the statements were false and defamatory. It claimed the publication stated Falwell "commits illegal, immoral and reprehensible acts, that he is an alcoholic and that he is insincere and hypo-critical in his work as a fundamentalist minister." The complaint alleged the statements were intended to bring "public hatred, contention, aversion and disgrace, and to induce an evil and unsavory opinion of him in the minds of the community." The last count was for intentional infliction of emotional distress and alleges "defendants acted willfully, intentionally, recklessly and maliciously, and their conduct was outrageous, extreme and intolerable in that it offends generally accepted standards of decency and morality." Damages sought were in the amount of $45,000,000.

The defense by Alan Isaacman, who represented Hustler Magazine in numerous lawsuits across the country, was based upon the argument that the ad was a joke because it was a parody of Compari Liqueur advertising on the one hand and on the other a satire of Falwell. Parody is the use of other language while satire refers to morals, manners, attitudes or behavior. Hence, the Hustler ad parodied the Compari ad and satirized Falwell.

The defense argued the ad actually communicated that Falwell was a hypocrite. Hustler's position was that no one could possibly believe that Falwell was an incestuous drunk who had sex with his mother before he preached. The defendant argued the First Amendment to the United States Constitution guarantees freedom of speech, freedom of the press and that objection to speech seen as obscene, indecent, or disgusting cannot be supported by law.

There was no question that if anyone needed the First Amendment protections it was Larry Flynt and Hustler Magazine. He had been prosecuted for sodomy, obscenity and contempt charges and had been sued hundreds of times for what he printed in Hustler Magazine. At the time of his deposition in the Falwell case, Flynt was incarcerated for contempt of court, was in pain, semi-paralyzed and frightening in appearance with his beard, bedsores and long hair. In addition, he was full of hatred since his companies had been put into a conservatorship being run by his brother whom he accursed of trying to take over his businesses. Since the deposition was to be videotaped, Flynt demanded his handcuffs be taken off before he would agree to take the oath. After much discussion it was agreed only his head and shoulders would show in the video. As the deposition continued, it became a circus. Flynt refused to answer questions. At one point a medical orderly from the prison entered the room and Flynt demanded medical treatment. At that time Grutman started questioning the medical attendant putting him under oath. After a couple of questions, Flynt started questioning the medical orderly and the lawyers did nothing but shout at each other.

Flynt was raised in a Kentucky mountain sharecropper's cabin, joined the Army at 14, married twice, declared bankruptcy before he became 21, and then opened a string of Hustler strip-joint bars in Ohio. The internal newsletter of these bars ultimately became Hustler Magazine with a circulation of over 2,000,000 and annual profits exceeding $10,000,000. He combined the unique slick-paper appearance of Playboy and Penthouse with disgusting art and copy. He delivered sex, hate and perversion in a manner that could be considered a parody of Playboy and Penthouse. His position was that those two magazines tried to deliver sex as art with sophisticated literature whereas Hustler Magazine was the real thing. He also operated legitimate newspapers and magazines through the Flynt Distributing Company, which actually was a defendant in this case initially, but was dismissed since no case was proven against it.

An attempted assassination of Flynt took place in Lawrenceville, Georgia in 1978. Two men fired a number of shots, wounding his lawyer and leaving Flynt paralyzed from the waist down. No one was ever arrested for the shooting and conspiracy theories abounded as to who wanted him dead. Since he had so many enemies, the investigation never narrowed to specific suspects. Flynt thought he was shot because of numerous questions he was asking in his magazine about John F. Kennedy's assassination. In 1984, he ran for President of the United States using the slogan "A Smut Peddler Who Cares." In addition to being sued frequently, Flynt brought numerous cases to the courts in his efforts to protect the First Amendment. He prevailed over the government who tried to stop his mailing Hustler Magazine to all members of Congress. He sued the government during the invasion of Granada because of the news blackout. That case became moot when the restriction was lifted. In 1983, Flynt yelled obscenities to Justices of the United States Supreme Court during an argument in one of his cases.

In his deposition, Flynt stated he was trying to get back at Falwell for his comments about Flynt's father and he claimed the statements in the parody were true. In fact, he stated he did not want to use the word parody in the ad but his lawyers made him do it. He agreed with Grutman that he wanted the ad to convey the truth. He wanted the ad to be taken seriously. He also agreed he was trying to convey that Falwell was a liar, a hypocrite and that he wanted to assassinate Falwell's integrity. The plaintiffs obtained the admissions they wanted to support their case and the statement by Flynt that he wanted to ruin Falwell's reputation certainly indicated malice.

Defamation in writing is libel. The statement must attack someone's reputation so that it negatively affects it within the community. It must be untrue because if it is true it is not defamation. The law in this area is convoluted because it is based on state common law as well as federal constitutional law. In the case of <u>New York Times Company v. Sullivan</u>, the United States Supreme Court restricted the power of states to award damages to plaintiffs in libel trials. The decision came in the early 1960's during the civil rights movement in the south. A southern jury awarded a Montgomery, Alabama police commissioner, L.B. Sullivan, $500,000 for the running of a paid advertisement by the Committee to Defend Martin Luther King. It was alleged the advertisement claimed southern racism and police brutality was used against Dr. King for pursuing the civil rights of blacks in the south. In his decision, Justice Brennan pointed out Sullivan was a member of the government, therefore criticizing him was the same as criticizing the government. To recover, the plaintiff would have to prove by clear and convincing evidence that the publication was with actual malice, defined as "knowledge of falsity" or "reckless disregard" for truth or falsity. The court made it clear this standard should not be confused with the common use of the word malice which normally means personal malice or hatred. Reckless disregard was more than stupidity or sloppiness. There must also exist actual doubt about the truth or falsity of the story. In subsequent cases the United States Supreme Court stated Sullivan not only applied to public officials but also to public figures. Hence Falwell, being a public figure, had to prove Hustler and Flynt had actual malice. There was no question, after Flynt's deposition, the plaintiff could prove common law malice, but was there "knowledge of or reckless disregard for falsity" in the context of the ad which claimed to be a parody?

Libel requires a misstatement of fact. An expression of opinion such as "Falwell is a hypocrite and I hate you" is an expression of opinion. Put another way, the ad was so outrageous that it was unbelievable, hence not factual, and therefore not libelous.

One species of the tort of invasion of privacy is the appropriation of name or likeness. This is actually a property right which has value. A celebrity's name and likeness has commercial value. Unfortunately for Falwell, it is obvious his name and likeness is not being used by Hustler Magazine to sell Compari Liqueur. Arguably it was being used to sell Hustler Magazine. However, case law holds a publication can use a public figure's likeness to illustrate a story without compensation.

The final cause of action, i.e., intentional infliction of emotional distress, is relatively new. It first arose in an English case during the 19th century when an individual told a woman her husband had been severely injured in an accident, causing her severe stress. The defendant actually thought it was a joke and his defense was, "Can't you take a joke?" The English court did not feel it was a laughing matter and imposed liability on the jokester. Since Falwell was a citizen of Virginia, the law of that state was applied. The law required the conduct be intentional or reckless, that it offend generally accepted standards of decency or morality, it must be causally connected to the plaintiff's emotional distress, and that such distress must be severe. It was the easier cause of action to prove in this case and had the least legal issues.

During the trial, the defense presented two motions to Judge Turk. The first was to preclude Flynt's deposition being used in evidence on the basis he was incompetent at the time it was taken. Initially, the Judge ruled for the defense because after reviewing the video it was obvious defendant Flynt was, not only by language but also appearance, a wild man. However, within a few days Judge Turk reversed himself and stated he would allow the use of the deposition.

The second motion was to disqualify plaintiff's counsel Grutman. It was alleged he paid a witness $10,000 for his testimony. The witness was Flynt's brother-in-law, Bill Rider, who until the year prior, when he was fired, was Hustler's chief of security. Grutman's position was he paid the $10,000 not only because it covered expenses and costs to the witness for the deposition and testimony at trial, but also because Rider did some pretrial investigative work in obtaining certain documents that the plaintiffs wanted to use to prove Flynt personally okayed the ad. The defense attorneys also presented Judge Turk with numerous other alleged examples of Grutman's problems with courts and supposedly unethical conduct. The Judge decided to allow Grutman to continue but warned him he would be watched.

Plaintiff's first witness in the trial was Jerry Falwell. He was born in 1933 in Virginia and lived in that state most of his life. "Since I became a Christian in 1952, I have been and am a teetotaler." Those were his words to support his unhappiness with being in a Compari liqueur ad. His father and grandfather were agnostics and it was not until after college, through the efforts of his mother, that he became a Christian. Attending Baptist Bible College in Springfield, Missouri, he became a minister. His mother passed away in 1977 approximately seven years before the trial. She was 82 at the time and according to Falwell she was a "saint." The defense stipulated his mother was a good person. Falwell defended his entry into politics because he needed to become involved in the moral issues of the times, i.e., abortion, gay rights, pornography, etc. He stated these matters influenced American culture and led him to form the "Moral Majority." It was this decision, to become both a religious and political leader, that caused many of Falwell's enemies, including Larry Flynt, to attack him. Falwell testified he had attempted to stamp out pornography "with every breath in my body."

The plaintiff testified regarding other stories about him which he had found in Hustler Magazine as well as other parodies. He specifically denied doing any of the things alleged in the ad which was the subject of this case. Also, he never drank Compari. He testified that when he first saw the ad he did not see the small print at the bottom stating it was not to be taken seriously. He then testified regarding the stress he incurred and suffered as a result of the ad. On cross-examination, he not only had to admit lying about a statement made during a meeting with President Jimmy Carter, but also he tried to explain away the alleged selling of blessings and various other inconsistencies which the defense wanted the jury to hear.

Since this was basically a case that only involved Falwell and Flynt, the next major witness was Flynt. He appeared in Roanoke well dressed and was well behaved. Knowing the jury would see some of the deposition testimony, Isaacman asked Flynt how he felt at the time of the deposition. Flynt gave a long answer referring to manic depression, stress and physical injury including the fact he had broken his leg two days before the deposition. He testified at length regarding his brother's attempt to take over his companies and basically tried to show the jury that the Larry Flynt they should pay attention to was the one in the courtroom and not the one in the deposition. He testified he did not intend the parody to have any effect on Falwell. He stated he was responding to his own readership and pointed out it was certainly unbelievable. He did a good job explaining the damaging deposition and his thinking that the ad satire was so outrageous that no one could possibly take it seriously.

On cross-examination, Grutman proceeded to differentiate between the Larry Flynt who was respectful and somewhat sympathetic in his wheelchair in the Roanoke courtroom versus the obscenity ridden individual who yelled at the Supreme Court of the United States on November 8, 1983. Since Flynt testified he did not normally use obscenities, Grutman proceeded to use other court transcripts wherein he did so. Although Isaacman tried to keep out of evidence an interview Flynt gave to Screw Magazine in 1975, it was used by Grutman and the content of it was so gross the jury could not help but determine Flynt's "parodies" were disgusting, outrageous and sick. The point Grutman got across to the jury was that Flynt's use of parody and satire was simply a way of covering up his perverted hatred and that he would say whatever he wanted, whenever he wanted, including listing Jesus H. Christ as the publisher of Hustler, calling Reverend Falwell a motha---and describing the Bible as a piece of excrement.

After the testimony was in, there was not much question regarding Falwell's case against Flynt and Hustler Magazine. The only real question was how much the jury would award. That was soon answered with $100,000 in compensatory damages and $50,000 in punitive damages each from the two defendants, a total award of $300,000. The verdict was appealed to the United States Court of Appeal for the Fourth Circuit which affirmed the judgment against Flynt and Hustler Magazine. The Court of Appeal rejected Flynt's and Hustler's arguments that the actual malice standard set forth in New York Times Company v. Sullivan had to be met before Falwell could recover for emotional distress. The Court of Appeal acknowledged that the ad parody did not describe actual facts and pointed out the jury so held. The Court felt that was irrelevant and the only issue is whether or not the publication was sufficiently outrageous to constitute intentional infliction of emotional distress.

The issue presented to the Supreme Court as set forth by Justice Rehnquist was: "We must decide whether a public figure may recover damages for emotional harm caused by the publication of an ad parody offensive to him, and doubtless gross and repugnant in the eyes of most." The United States Supreme Court overturned the Fourth Circuit Court of Appeal's position that a state interest in protecting public persons from emotional distress is sufficient to deny First Amendment protection to speech that is patently offensive and is intended to inflict emotional injury even when that speech could not have been reasonably interpreted as stating actual facts about the public figure involved.

Justice Rehnquist pointed out that the First Amendment encourages robust political debate and that as such is bound to be at times critical of those who hold public office or those public figures who are intimately involved in the resolution of important public questions. One of the perogatives of American citizenship is the right to criticize public men in their positions. Sometimes that criticism will be "vehement, caustic, and sometimes unpleasantly sharp..."

In summary, the Court held the First Amendment trumps state court liability and that political cartoons, parody and satire have their place in American discourse in publications. "Outrageousness is not a standard because the public expression of ideas may not be prohibited merely if they themselves are offensive. Public figures and public officials may not recover damages for the tort of intentional infliction of emotional distress because of the publication of words, as in this case, without showing in addition the words are false and were made with actual malice or with reckless disregard as to whether or not the words were true. Since the jury found the ad parody could not "reasonably be understood as describing actual facts or actual events in which Falwell participated", the publication was not of facts which were false and made with actual malice or reckless disregard.

CHAPTER 14

GENERAL WILLIAM C. WESTMORELAND v. CBS AND MIKE WALLACE AND GENERAL ARIEL SHARON v. TIME MAGAZINE

IN THESE TWO CASES of the "Generals," did the defendants, CBS television and/or Time Magazine, act negligently and/or with reckless disregard in the preparation and presentation of stories regarding the plaintiffs?

In the case of General William C. Westmoreland, Commander of the United States forces in Vietnam from 1964 to 1968, CBS produced a 90 minute television show presented to the public in January 1982. The title of the production was "The Uncounted Enemy: A Vietnam Deception." It alleged that a conspiracy existed at the highest levels of the American military to continue support for the war within Congress, the executive branch of government, and the general public.

General Ariel Sharon brought an action against Time Magazine because of a statement in its cover story on February 21, 1983 which stated Sharon, who at the time was the Israeli Defense Minister, was responsible for the September 1982 Christian Phalangist killing of Palestinian refugees in the Sabra and Shatila refugee camps near Beirut.

It was alleged Sharon supported the Phalangist's retaliation against the Palestinians because of the killing of their leader, Bashir Gemayel.

Both cases went to trial at the federal courthouse in Foley Square, New York City, at the same time. Interestingly, the defense lawyers in both cases were from the same law firm, Cravath, Swaine & Moore. The judges in both cases had to advise jurors not to be affected by any rumors or other statements they heard regarding the other case. Both cases were extensively covered by the press and, of course, all members of the media had an interest in seeing the First Amendment used as a defense against the lawsuits. Initially, both plaintiffs had to prove statements made were knowingly false and were made with reckless disregard. That was the standard set down by the United States Supreme Court in New York Times v. Sullivan. In that case, a public official who was a police commissioner, could not obtain compensation for libel unless it was proven, not only that the charge against him was false, but that it was published with either actual malice or with reckless disregard for the truth.

Westmoreland complained that CBS, in its January 23, 1982 broadcast, alleged he had used deception in 1967 by intentionally providing intelligence estimates reflecting far fewer enemy troops than were actually present in South Vietnam. It was further alleged that during a long period before the January 30, 1968 Tet offensive, he deliberately reduced intelligence estimates of the number of North Vietnamese troops entering South Vietnam. Immediately following the airing of the report, the popular press, including the New York Times, reported the CBS allegations as the truth and in fact most of the American public accepted the allegations, notwithstanding the fact numerous public officials, including General Westmoreland, quickly issued denials and rebuttals.

Some months later, two investigative reporters, Don Kowet and Sally Bedell published in TV Guide a journalistic analysis of the show "The Uncounted Enemy: A Vietnam Deception." Their story was entitled "Anatomy of a Smear" and the article proceeded to set forth numerous errors and misrepresentations. CBS immediately undertook an internal investigation, the results of which were never published. General Westmoreland brought suit against CBS for libel. Generally, the public treated Mike Wallace and his associate, George Crile, as victims although there were some individuals in the media who believed the CBS presentation was susceptible to attack.

On February 21, 1983, Time Magazine published a cover story "Verdict on the Massacre," reporting on the findings of an Israeli commission investigating responsibility for the killing of several hundred civilians in Palestinian refugee camps. As part of the story, a paragraph was included referring to Appendix B which had not been published for security reasons. The paragraph purported to state intelligence agents reported Sharon encouraged Christian Phalangist forces to go into the Palestinian refugee camps to take revenge for the assassination of Bashir Gemayel.

World wide media quickly picked up on this allegation and repeated it. Shortly thereafter a member of the Israel parliament, who had access to Appendix B, advised a Time correspondent the magazine was mistaken and that there was no mention of the accusation in that Appendix. The Time correspondent reported to his superior in New York, and later testified in deposition, he did not think that was news. He made no further effort to investigate, check or confirm. The correspondent stated he was suspicious of the member of parliament because he would have been violating Israeli law by confiding "to me what is essentially a big secret," namely the context of Appendix B.

Because of the New York Times v. Sullivan holding, attorneys must have advised both of the "Generals" that their claims of libel would be very difficult to prove. Not only would they have to prove the statements were false, but they would have to prove they were made with actual malice or in reckless disregard for the truth. Unlike the law in many countries wherein the publication must prove what they allege is true, in the United States the plaintiff must prove the statements are false. That puts a very heavy burden on plaintiffs in libel actions, especially in the type of cases presented by the "Generals." They were both certainly public officials covered by the <u>Sullivan</u> case.

Westmoreland was offered help by the Capital Legal Foundation, a conservative group that normally opposes governmental regulation of business. Their attorney, Daniel M. Burt, a lawyer with no trial experience, took up Westmoreland's cause. Milton S. Gould, a highly experienced trial lawyer from the firm of Shea & Gould, represented Ariel Sharon. The Cravath firm fielded a very aggressive and experienced defense attorney, Thomas D. Barr, to represent Time Magazine and David Boies, an experienced partner, to represent CBS. Boies subsequently became famous representing the Democratic party in the Bush versus Gore election controversy. The defendants moved for summary judgment in both cases stating they believed there was no real issue of material fact to be decided and both motions failed. Discovery proceeded in the cases and of course the resources of the defendant media companies far exceeded those of the plaintiffs.

On October 31, 1984, Judge Leval started the <u>Westmoreland v. CBS</u> trial. Judge Sofaer started the <u>Sharon v. Time</u> matter at the same time. In the <u>Westmoreland</u> case there were 12 jurors and six alternates. In the <u>Sharon</u> case, six jurors were impaneled with five alternates. Westmoreland sued for over $100,000,000 and Sharon for $50,000,000, figures obviously fixed by their lawyers. General Westmoreland stated any monetary recovery would go to charity. His trial took four months while the <u>Sharon</u> case was concluded in two and a half months.

Both plaintiffs were called upon to prove that they did not do what they were accused of doing which is actually proving a negative. That is very difficult to accomplish. The plaintiffs wanted to uphold their honor, the defendants wanted to protect the First Amendment and the lawyers wanted to prevail. The cases were notorious because they involved the courts, lawyers, the press and the military, all powerful constituencies in the United States.

The CBS exposé relied greatly on an individual named Samuel A. Adams, a young intelligence analyst who had been with the CIA during the Vietnam War. Because he testified in the trial of Daniel Ellsberg, he had become known and sought after as an individual, supporting the theory of numerous Vietnam War cover-ups. Westmoreland became a target of Adams who developed information about Westmoreland and tried to have him court-martialed. Adams believed Westmoreland had engaged in a conspiracy with others to cover up enemy troop estimates and that he felt there were twice as many North Vietnamese troops and Viet Cong supporters in South Vietnam than the military estimates. Adams' conspiracy to deceive position really was not based on facts. What was at issue were estimates of enemy strength at certain times and the inclusion of villagers as Viet Cong.

The main military witnesses at trial were General McChristian and Colonel Hawkins. They were both intelligence officers stationed at the Saigon headquarters during 1966 and 1967. The defense obtained a concession from them, especially Colonel Hawkins, that indicated General Westmoreland had put a level on North Vietnamese soldiers and Viet Cong supporters at approximately 300,000. There should have been no surprise regarding the testimony of these officers because in his opening statement David Boies pointed out they had been deposed and he had given the jury an indication of their testimony. Westmoreland's attorney, Daniel Burt, and the media made it appear the testimony was a surprise. It was obvious that General Westmoreland was demoralized by the damaging testimony of his former subordinates and shortly thereafter the trial was "discontinued" by the issuance of a joint statement prepared by the plaintiff and the defendants. Issued on February 19, 1985, approximately six weeks into the defendants' presentation of its case, it set forth that because of the trial, the matters set forth in the broadcast of January 23, 1982 had been extensively examined, that both parties believed their actions broadened the public record on this matter and that both sides believed they had presented their position to the public for consideration.

CBS stated it respected General Westmoreland's long and faithful service to his country and never intended to assert and did not in fact believe he was unpatriotic or disloyal in the performance of his duties as he saw them. General Westmoreland stated he respected the long and distinguished journalistic tradition of CBS, the rights of journalists who examined the complex issues of Vietnam and the prerogative to present perspectives contrary to his own. The matter never went to the jury so it would be speculative to determine what would have been their decision. Probably, a motion for directed verdict would have been made by CBS at the end of its case, and because of the plaintiff's difficult burden of proof, that the motion may well have been granted.

Ariel Sharon's case against Time concluded with a verdict in favor of Sharon finding Time had defamed him by printing a false story. However, the jury concluded the reporter had been negligent and careless rather than malicious or reckless and no monetary award was granted.

Judge Sofaer had asked the government of Israel to provide, under seal, information relevant to the trial. The only stipulation the Israelis put on the provision was it be furnished only to the court, the lawyers and the jury. They alone had access to all the documents relating to Appendix B and that Appendix itself. Hence Judge Sofaer excluded the public and the press when the information was produced. By agreement a witness to the Appendix was allowed to answer three questions, yes or no. If any answer was yes, the plaintiff would lose. The questions were: "Does the document contain any evidence or suggestion that Minister Sharon had any discussion with the

Phalangist in which either person mentioned the need for revenge?"; "Does the document contain any evidence or suggestion that Minister Sharon had a discussion with the Gemayel family or with any other Phalangist... in which Minister Sharon discussed the need to avenge the death of Bashir Gemayel?"; "Does the document contain any evidence or suggestion that Minister Sharon knew in advance that the Phalangist would massacre the civilians if they went into the camps unaccompanied by I.D.F. troops?" The answer to all three questions was no.

At the conclusion of this evidence, Judge Sofaer submitted the case to the jury with a charge based on the Sullivan case. Actually, the Judge's instructions were convoluted and very difficult to understand. Realizing this, the Judge agreed to provide a manuscript of the charge to the jury for its consideration.

The jury was then asked to answer the following questions: "Was the paragraph concerning Sharon defamatory, and if it was defamatory, was the defamation aggravated by its attribution to Appendix B?" This was followed by a question regarding whether or not the jury found the falsity had been proven by clear and convincing evidence, and then questions with regard to whether or not the publication was with actual malice, i.e., with knowledge that it was false or with reckless disregard as to whether it was false or not, or with serious doubt that it was true.

In summary, the jury had to determine if statements in the paragraph were false, hence whether or not Sharon had been defamed, and if so, was that proven by clear and convincing evidence. They then had to decide whether all of the subsequent elements had been proven before damages could be awarded.

The jury in this case was highly intelligent and organized. It requested a blackboard, cough medicine, three ring binders, file folders, chalk, portions of transcripts and a good dictionary. They wanted to know if they were working over the weekend and whether or not heat would be provided (it was January in New York and cold). Two days later, on January 16, 1985, the jury foreman announced that the jury had concluded the statements in the paragraph were false and that the plaintiff had proven they were false by clear and convincing evidence. The Judge then asked them to proceed and answer the other questions. After 11 days of deliberations, the jury found that while the preparers of the article were negligent, it determined the statements were made without actual malice, and that at the time of the publication the authors did not know the statements were false, nor did they have serious doubts as to their truthfulness.

Both cases show that any plaintiff who is a public official or a notable individual will have a very heavy burden to prove defamation and recover successfully against the media in the United States. By becoming public personalities, individuals become fair game for critical comment and even negligent allegations or misrepresentations. We, as members of the public, should understand that just because an individual does not sue a publisher for defamatory statements, that does not mean the statements published are true. They may be true or they may be false and we must recognize that no recovery is allowed a public figure even though they are in fact defamed by false statements absent all the other elements needed under New York Times v. Sullivan. Reckless disregard amounting to malice is very difficult to prove. The First Amendment rules supreme.

The media and the public must now be aware it is possible an obscure individual can be launched into the national spotlight in a matter of hours and the media who did so should not then be able to rely on New York Times v. Sullivan as a defense to a libel or defamation action. The media should not boot strap itself using its own publicity to advance the argument the individual is now a well-known person or a celebrity.

CHAPTER 15

Rice v. Paladin enterprises, inc.

PALADIN PRESS AND ITS publisher Peter Lund printed and sold
a murder-for-hire instruction manual entitled "Hit Man: A Technical
Manual for Independent Contractors". The 1983 publication was a
state of the art, detailed, step-by-step, technical, manual for becoming
a professional hit man, with chapters on planning and carrying out
murders. It encouraged the reader to become a cold blooded murderer.

Lawrence Horn hired James Perry to murder his crippled eight
year old son, Trevor Horn, his ex-wife Mildred Horn, as well as nurse
Janice Saunders. On the night of March 3, 1993, Perry, a hit man from
Detroit, did the job which he had planned using instructions contained
in Paladin's Hit Man manual.

Trevor Horn had been born prematurely resulting in numerous
medical problems. While hospitalized in 1985, a tube supplying
oxygen was accidentally displaced causing paralysis and brain damage,
necessitating constant medical care. Horn brought a lawsuit against the
hospital for malpractice. He recovered a multi-million dollar settlement
enabling Trevor to have constant care. His mother, Mildred Horn,
worked as a flight attendant and was away from home approximately
two to three days a week. Her sister, Vivian Elaine Rice, lived nearby

their Silver Springs, Maryland home and regularly checked on Trevor and his nurse. Elaine, following her usual habit, stopped at the Horn home early one morning to check on how things were going, and seeing the garage door open and hearing Trevor's respirator alarm beeping, knew something was wrong. Finding her sister's body just inside the front door, she ran out and asked someone to call the police. When they arrived they found the body of Mildred Horn near the front door and the bodies of Trevor Horn and nurse Janice Saunders in the house. The two adults had each been shot in the head multiple times with one shot through an eye into the brain. Trevor's respirator tube was detached and he died from lack of oxygen. It appeared the perpetrator(s) had entered through a patio door. Although there were signs a burglary was committed, i.e., bookcases moved and toppled, drawers opened, etc., the investigating detective concluded, because various pieces of jewelry and other valuable items had not been taken, that the alleged burglary was an attempt to cover up premeditated murders. There was little physical evidence, hence the police concentrated on motive rather than method. After investigating the family, the police soon zeroed in on Lawrence Horn. Under Maryland law, if his former wife and son died he would inherit the multi-million trust fund and that was sufficient motive for the detective.

Excellent police work, including investigating hotel registrations in the vicinity of the murders, revealed a man named James Perry had checked into a Days Inn, paid cash, but did use his driver's license for identification. Telephone records of Lawrence Horn showed he had received phone calls shortly before and after the murders from public telephones in the vicinity of the hotel and murder site. Checking further on Perry, the police learned he had various felony convictions for assault and armed robbery. Telephone records also showed a trail of phone calls between pay phones near Lawrence Horn's Los Angeles residence and pay phones near Perry's Detroit hangouts. With the help of Detroit police and the FBI, Detective Wittenberg of the Montgomery County Maryland police obtained wire tap and search warrants for Perry's home. When executing the search warrant police found numerous magazines and publications on crime and weapons. The detective called a number of the publishing companies to ascertain if Perry had purchased other materials. Upon contacting Paladin Press in Boulder, Colorado, he learned Perry had purchased two books, "How to Make Disposable Silencers" and "Hit Man: A Technical Manual for Independent Contractors". Police had determined the .22 caliber weapon used in the murders was equipped with a silencer.

Wittenberg read the Hit Man manual which stated the .22 caliber AR-7 gun was the best weapon for contract kills. A piece of an AR-7 rifle had been found by police near the murder scene along with Mildred Horn's credit cards. The book had also advised the reader to drill out the serial numbers on the weapon. The serial numbers on the parts of the rifle police found had been completely drilled through. The book advised potential killers to use a rat-tail file to scour the inside of the gun barrel to defeat ballistics tracings. Near the credit cards, police also found a rat-tail file with traces of gun powder on it. The book gave detailed instructions on how to build a silencer for the AR-7. The book advised firing from a distance of 3 to 6 feet and that at least one shot should go into the eye and into the brain. All of this fit the murders perfectly. Detective Wittenberg concluded that whoever killed Trevor, Mildred and Janice had read the book which also explained how to go into the business of murder-for-hire, how to find clients, negotiate contracts and determine what to charge. The suggested retail price for killing a federal judge was $250,000, and a county sheriff was between $75,000 and $100,000. It explained how to plan ahead, determine the mark's routines, assess the best place to do the deed and proper methods of surveillance. It made the point that killing was the easy part. The important work was making sure neither you nor your employer could be linked to the crime. That is what made the murderer a professional. It taught how to make bombs, dispose of bodies, how to collect your fee and finally how to retire. Attorney Rod Smolla, a well known defender of First Amendment rights, particularly in the area of publications, found the book to be evil incarnate. After a jury trial for first degree murder, Perry and Lawrence Horn were convicted. The book "Hit Man" was central to their being convicted.

A civil suit was filed in Federal District Court by surviving family members of the Horn and Saunders families. The defendants were Paladin Press and its publisher, Peter Lund. It alleged the defendants aided and abetted murders committed by James Perry and Lawrence Horn. Because Elaine Rice, Mildred's sister, was listed first in the court papers, the lawsuit became known as Rice v. Paladin Enterprises, Inc. Because of its uniqueness, the suit received a fair amount of press and television reporting. The defendants hired two well known First Amendment lawyers, Lee Levine and Tom Kelly. They promptly denounced the suit as censorship. Plaintiffs' counsel, on the other hand, had reviewed a series of three cases against Soldier of Fortune magazine. That magazine had printed advertisements that in two of the cases were explicit "gun for hire" ads. In one case a federal appeals court held that it would be too onerous and burdensome for publishers to reject all ambiguous ads. However, in a Georgia case, a multi-million dollar verdict was upheld because the ad was explicit. Rice's counsel felt Paladin's ads were so explicit there could be no doubt they were selling a how-to-do-it murder manual. Although much of the publishing world was aghast at Rod Smolla's being involved with the plaintiffs in this case because of his prior defense of publisher's rights under the First Amendment. *The Washington Post*, having reviewed the Hit Man manual, published an editorial stating that if the plaintiffs could prove what they had alleged, the First Amendment should not protect Paladin. Stuart Taylor Jr. wrote for the American Lawyer magazine, "I like my freedom of speech as well as the next fellow, but I'm with Smolla on this one…. A murder manual intentionally marketed to would be contract killers (along with assorted fantasists and others) doesn't strike me as the kind of 'freedom of speech' that the framers sought to protect."

The attorneys agreed to reverse the process of a normal trial. Rather than try the case on the facts and then apply the law, they agreed to do what is known as a "joint statement of facts" wherein each side negotiated and included what they believed the facts to be. The defendants agreed to include much of what the plaintiffs alleged, provided the plaintiffs allowed that the books they sold were also sold to people who would not commit crimes. The defense conceded it had "engaged in a marketing strategy intended to attract criminals and would-be criminals who desire information and instructions on how to commit crimes." Paladin also conceded "in publishing, distributing and selling Hit Man and silencers to Perry, defendants assisted him in the subsequent perpetration of the murders." The defendants thought that by obtaining the stipulation that its books were sold to writers, law enforcement officials, those who enjoy reading accounts of crime and the means for committing them, criminologists and others who would use the books lawfully, that they would win the case. The plaintiffs felt that the stipulation they had obtained, which in essence took away the issue of causation, would result in their winning the case.

Because of public interest in the issues involved, various organizations requested to file amicus curiae (friend of the court) briefs. Judge Alexander Williams of the Federal District Court for Maryland refused to accept the briefs.

Plaintiffs' attorneys were concerned that Judge Williams might consider this case as being covered by <u>Falwell v. Larry Flynt and Hustler Magazine</u> in that it was an effort to prosecute Paladin for its bad taste and disgusting views. The plaintiffs had to argue Hit Man was not teaching anything in the abstract but in fact was preparing individuals to commit illegal acts.

During arguments to Judge Williams, the defense stated Hit Man had redeeming value in that it was equally likely to persuade individuals not to enter the profession of being a paid assassin. He argued Paladin did not intend the book to be used by people to commit murder, only that Paladin knew it was possible such a person would follow the techniques described and kill someone. But, he pointed out that was true of many other novels, movies, etc.

Plaintiffs argued they were not relying on the fact the book was revolting and morally repugnant. The suit was not about ideas but about compensation for physical injury resulting from the murders it helped cause. Rod Smolla threw back at Tom Kelly the stipulation regarding the intent of the publications and pointed out he was now arguing against the stipulation.

Since the Judge had to decide a motion for summary judgment brought by the defendants on the basis their publication was protected by the First Amendment, he accepted the defense position and ruled against the plaintiffs.

As the plaintiffs' attorneys prepared their appeal to the Fourth Circuit Court of Appeals in Richmond, Virginia, the defense attorneys gathered support from numerous organizations supporting freedom of speech and freedom of the press. They lined up a number of amicus curiae briefs to support their position. The plaintiffs' attorneys were unable to garner much support for their position until, out of the blue, they were contacted by the United States Department of Justice. At that time, the Department was trying to ascertain for itself how far the government could go in censoring publications that taught others how to make bombs. A federal law passed in 1968 stated:

> "Whoever teaches or demonstrates to any other person the use, application, or making of any firearm or explosive or incendiary device, or technique capable of causing injury or death to persons, knowing or having reason to know or intending that the sale being unlawfully employed for use in, or in furtherance of, civil disorder which in any way or degree obstruct, delay, or adversely effect commerce or the movement of any article or commodity in commerce or the conduct or performance of any federally protected function... shall be fined not more than $10,000 or imprisoned not more than five years or both."

The Chicago Seven were accused of violating the statute and although their convictions were ultimately reversed on other grounds, federal courts had held in two other cases that the statute did not violate the First Amendment.

At oral arguments before Justices Williams W. Wilkens, Jr., Karen J. Williams and J. Michael Luttig, plaintiffs argued the publication Hit Man aided and abetted the commission of the crime. At least one of the justices, Luttig, seemed to have almost memorized the book and was clearly incensed by it. He felt the book was an incitement to commit crime as well as aiding, meaning to provide knowledge, and abetting, which means encouragement to potential criminals. Justice Luttig was unusually involved in the case and was very unsympathetic to the arguments of the defense. After oral arguments, Rod Smolla did some research and found that Justice Luttig was, himself, the victim of a murder. His father had been cruelly killed by teenagers in Texas.

It was not surprising that the Court of Appeals' decision rendered on November 10, 1997 was authored by Judge Michael Luttig who, reportedly, was on the short list for appointment to the U.S. Supreme Court in 2005. He wrote that the record amply supported the allegations the publication aided and abetted James Perry in his commission of the murders. Using the stipulations entered into by the parties and dissecting the Hit Man manual, Judge Luttig picked apart the defense argument that publication of the book was protected by the First Amendment.

After Paladin requested a rehearing before the entire 15 Judge Fourth Circuit Court of Appeals and was denied, it filed its appeal to the Supreme Court of the United States. Since the Fourth Circuit had overturned the trial judge's granting of defendants' motion for summary judgment, discovery in the case could proceed while the matter was pending before the United States Supreme Court.

Discovery revealed the original submission by the author proposed the article as a fictional account of a hit man's life. It was Paladin that wrote back suggesting the account be made into non-fiction in an instructional how to do it format. An addendum to the contract required Paladin to indemnify the author in the event of any liability resulting from material contained in the book. The defendants refused to identify the author, however plaintiffs learned her identity by other means. Plaintiffs' information was corroborated by the defendants, failure to black out the author's name on one page in the middle of the manuscript. When publisher Lund was deposed, this evidence was used and it created much acrimony between the defense counsel and their client. In the deposition, plaintiffs' attorneys took Lund through the Paladin Press catalog and questioned him regarding numerous books and publications discussing how to make flame throwers, poisons, bombs, etc. One publication even addressed a method to test poison by finding a wino in an urban area and trying it out him. Lund agreed Paladin would sell Muammar Qaddafi (this is before Qaddafi's alleged conversion) production materials for semtex if he mailed in for it. It was pointed out that Timothy McVeigh, the Okalahoma Federal Building bomber, had purchased books on how to make explosives from Paladin Press.

Eventually, the Supreme Court of the United States denied the defendants' petition for hearing thereby upholding the Fourth Circuit Court of Appeals' decision. As the case came close to trial before Judge Williams in Maryland during June 1998, the Columbine High School shootings took place, followed closely by six students being wounded in a school shooting in Conyers, Georgia. This put pressure on Paladin and its insurance company, which had been defending under a reservations of its rights and, just before the case was to start trial, a multi-million dollar settlement was reached that included yearly contributions to two charities of the plaintiffs' choice. Some funds went to the victims of the Littleton Colorado school shootings and to the victims of the Oklahoma City Federal Building bombing. Paladin agreed to take the book Hit Man off the market and not sell it in the future.

Some defenders of the First Amendment find this case disturbing. In a case known as Byers v. Edmonson, a Louisiana Appellate Court held that the victims of a convenience store shooting could proceed against the producers of the film Natural Born Killers, its producer, Warner Bros., and its director, Oliver Stone. The theory was the perpetrators of the shooting had gone on a crime and shooting spree after seeing the movie. The suit alleged the producers knew and intended that the film would inspire persons to engage in such crime and violence. While the film's producers tried to have the case thrown out of court on First Amendment grounds, the appellate court, using the decision of Judge

Luttig in the "Hit Man" case, allowed the case to proceed. This case is probably frivolous and eventually the defendants will prevail. In <u>Byers,</u> the defense attorneys moved for a judgment on the pleadings. Using that procedure the Judge must assume the allegations are true. Had they moved for summary judgment as Paladin did in the <u>Rice</u> case and argued there was no proof of the necessary deliberate intent, they may well have prevailed. Peter Lund at Paladin Press knew that some people bought his book "Hit Man" to learn how to murder, some did and he knew some would. That is deliberate intent, sufficient to show reckless disregard and the requisite malice. Finally, a powerful Federal Appellate Court drew a line bright enough to warn others.

CHAPTER 16

ROE V. WADE

IN THE EARLY 1970'S, Norma McCorvey (Jane Roe) met two lawyers at Colombo's Pizza restaurant in Dallas. The first lawyer to arrive was 26-year old Linda Coffee. Subsequently, an older and more senior attorney, Sarah Weddington, arrived and the three discussed Norma's need for an abortion. This landmark case started out unpretentiously. Factually, it was based on lies. Norma McCorvey told the lawyers she was pregnant as a result of being raped in Georgia by three men while she was employed with a traveling circus. She wanted to obtain counsel and hoped to do so by engendering sympathy; hence, she invented the story and admitted doing so years after the court's decision. In an interesting twist, she is now an anti-abortionist. Having been turned down for an abortion by a couple of physicians she was somewhat desperate. Both lawyers had been looking for a case in which to invalidate the Texas abortion laws. At that time, approximately 8,000 to 10,000 legal abortions were performed in the United States each year. Experts opined there were between 1 million and 1.5 million abortions performed annually. It was well known that women who obtained illegal abortions were put at much greater risk than those able to obtain legal abortions. Both lawyers were motivated primarily by their ideology. Neither one

167

had any personal connection with abortion. However, they had what Norma McCorvey was looking for, and that was disdain for the Texas statutes. Linda Coffee was reportedly a quiet, contemplative woman while Sarah Weddington was more outgoing and Norma liked her immediately. As it developed, Linda prepared the pleadings and Sarah handled the arguments.

The lawyers contemplated how to attack the statutes and finally decided to bring a class action for declaratory relief against the District Attorney of Dallas County, Henry Wade, seeking an injunction to preclude the District Attorney from prosecuting anyone who performed an abortion. Initially, the attorneys had to concern themselves with what is known as "standing to sue" issues, so they enlarged the suit to include a doctor by the name of Hallford and a childless married couple known as the "Does". Their claim was based on future injury that could result from contraceptive failure, pregnancy, unpreparedness for parenthood or impairment of the wife's health. By bringing the case in the Federal District Court alleging Texas statutes were unconstitutional, the plaintiffs were able to obtain a trial by a three-judge panel from which it was possible to take a direct appeal to the United States Supreme Court. The relatively inexperienced lawyers handled the procedural matters extremely well and accomplished their goals in an expeditious manner.

The three judge District Court panel granted declaratory relief holding the Texas abortion statutes unconstitutional. However, the Court refused the plaintiff's request for an injunction against the District Attorney of Dallas County. This resulted in Henry Wade not being precluded from prosecuting physicians who allegedly committed abortions while the declaratory relief decision was on appeal to the United States Supreme Court. Wade, who had become famous for his involvement in the President John F. Kennedy assassination/Lee Harvey Oswald matter and the prosecution of Jack Ruby, decided to continue bringing charges against abortion doctors. This allowed the plaintiffs to appeal the three-judge panel's decision not to issue an injunction to the United States Supreme Court and set the stage for the "woman's right to choose decision."

The Texas abortion statute enacted in 1859 was considered to be an "old-style" law versus reform laws that were passed in the 1960's. The Texas law was very restrictive and permitted abortion only to save the mother's life. It did not allow abortion in cases of incest or rape. The newer statutes typically allowed therapeutic exceptions dealing with the mother's physical or mental health, the prevention of serious fetal deformity or to the termination of a pregnancy resulting from rape or incest. These newer statutes were supposed to make abortion more widely available; however, because of administrative procedures and other requirements based on residence, age, consent for minors, some argued they actually hindered the abortion process. Weddington and Coffee challenged the constitutionality of Articles 1191 through 1194 and 1196 of the Texas Abortion Law. Abortion was defined as "the destruction of the life of the fetus or embryo in the woman's womb or causing premature birth for that purpose." It called for confinement in a penitentiary for not less than two nor more than five years if done with consent, and if done without consent, the punishment was doubled. Should the death of the mother occur during an abortion, it would be classified as a murder. The only exception was set forth in Article 1196 and that was to save the life of the mother.

The three-judge District Court panel held that the fundamental right of single women and married persons to choose whether to have children is protected by the 9th and 14th Amendments to the U.S. Constitution and that the Texas criminal abortion statutes were void because they were both unconstitutionally vague and were an overbroad infringement of the plaintiff's 9th Amendment rights. The Court found that Norma McCorvey and members of her class as well as Dr. Hallford had standing to bring the action but the childless couple known as the Does failed to state facts sufficient to present a controversy; hence, they did not have standing. However, the Court's refusal to issue an injunction allowed that part of the District Court's judgment to be directly appealed to the highest court in the land. The defendant district attorney cross-appealed from the Court's granting of declaratory relief to Norma McCorvey and Dr. Hallford.

The United States Supreme Court's handling of this matter was closely watched. Chief Justice Warren Burger was just beginning to establish himself on the Court and Justice Harry Blackmun was added at the end of the 1970 term by President Richard Nixon. There was concern President Nixon was determined to politicize the Court much as Franklin Roosevelt was accused of doing in the 1930's. With the deaths of justices Hugo Black and John Marshall Harlan, in the fall of 1971, President Nixon had the opportunity to make good on his campaign pledge to restrain the growing liberality of the Court.

Chief Justice Warren Burger, a supporter of state's rights, initially seemed to favor upholding state abortion laws, but also indicated he thought the Texas law might be vague. Justice White was adamant the law should be supported. In opposition were Justices Douglas, Marshall and Brennan who seemed willing to acknowledge the constitutional right to abortion. Justices Stewart and Blackmun, who were considered centrists, apparently favored striking some, but not all of the Texas abortion laws.

At the time, there were only seven justices sitting on the Supreme Court. It was the custom at the Court for the senior justice in the majority to assign the writing of the opinion; however, after the conference vote was taken, Justice Douglas, the senior justice in the majority, was shocked to find Chief Justice Burger had assigned the opinion to

Justice Blackmun. Since both Burger and Blackmun were from the same neighborhood in St. Paul, they were known as the "Minnesota Twins." Justice Douglas believed Chief Justice Burger misused the rules in an effort to circumvent the majority. It was well known that Justice Douglas had been waiting for an abortion case for some years and was clearly ready to rule a woman's right to privacy gave her the choice. He also knew Justice Blackmun viewed the issue as one concerning abortion laws restricting a doctor's right to practice medicine. Burger responded to Douglas' written memorandum asserting his right to assign the case by taking the position the conference vote was too vague to determine a clear majority. Therefore, he felt free to assign the opinion himself. Chief Justice Burger refused to back down; hence, the opinion would be written by Justice Blackmun. This relatively junior justice had considered becoming a physician himself but opted for the law. He had been the general counsel at the Mayo Clinic in Rochester, Minnesota, and because of this "medical background" he thought he was uniquely prepared to write the opinion and understand the complicated issues involved. He was also very pleased to be given such a controversial case since normally new justices are given simpler matters. It also developed that he became the Court's most meticulous worker, although his detractors felt he was simply slow. Numerous amicus curiae briefs were filed in the case. The seasons changed from fall to winter and then to spring before Blackmun finally circulated a draft opinion in mid-May. He came down on the side of striking the abortion laws. He went through a lengthy recitation of the history of abortion, a lengthy discussion of viability and the state's compelling interest in protecting the fetus, but he did not address what others thought was the real issue, that being the right of a woman to do what she wished with her body. Justice Douglas was pleased Blackmun had at least joined his camp on this crucial issue. Justices Marshall, Brennan and Stewart soon joined the majority. Justices Burger and White were in the minority.

In late May, Justices Lewis Powell and William Rehnquist were seated on the Court and a move was made to put the matter over for reargument to the next term thereby allowing those justices to take part in the decision. Justice Douglas became very frustrated and felt Burger did this for political reasons. Douglas knew that had he not backed down on his right to assign the written opinion, which he would have assigned to himself, a decision would have been made months earlier and the matter would have already been decided. Douglas made an attempt to change the situation and even hinted he would go public. After Justice Blackmun assured him they would retain the majority notwithstanding the two new justices just appointed by President Nixon, he capitulated and conformed with the Court's custom not to air its differences in public. It was felt Rehnquist would not join them, but possibly Powell would.

Continuing the case to the next term caused much public speculation that the Court would not strike the state laws and that President Nixon's appointees joining the Court would make it more reluctant to change state criminal laws.

Finally, on the following January 22, Justice Blackmun read a summary of his majority opinion which initially dealt in detail with medical issues. He finally addressed a woman's right to privacy, finding the abortion laws violated the 14th Amendment's concept of personal liberty and the 9th Amendment's reservation of rights to the people. The pro-choice forces had won. A woman's right to an abortion was constitutionally protected.

However, Blackmun's opinion held a woman's right to privacy was not absolute and that a state's intrusion might be based upon moral reasons, protection of woman's health, or protection of potential life.

Since the State of Texas had not raised the aforementioned exceptions, they were not discussed in detail. The second was clearly based on Blackmun's medical background, but the third exception surprised many in as much as Blackmun had created the concept of protection of potential life. He then went on to find the Court did not have to resolve the difficult question of when life begins and that there was no consensus, therefore, the Court would not speculate as to the answer. He then specifically addressed how states could intervene, describing the different stages of pregnancy. In the first trimester, the State could not intervene, in the second, it could intervene to protect a woman's health, and in the third, it could intervene to protect the life of a viable fetus.

Justices White and Rehnquist read their dissents. Normally, dissents were not read because it was not a friendly thing to do to another justice. However, Justice White was scathing in his views, while Rehnquist was less adamant. He opposed the decision as being 'judicial legislation' primarily addressing the third trimester division of pregnancy. Chief Justice Warrant Burger joined the majority, although he did so in a terse manner, pointing out the Court rejected any claim that the Constitution requires abortions on demand. Justice Stewart's opinion, concurring with Justice Blackmun, was surprising to many since he had held the opposite in an earlier case and considered himself to be a strong defender of stari decisis (follow prior law). One explanation may have been his wife's strong disagreement with his decision in the prior case, since she was a member of Planned Parenthood and was reportedly very upset about his earlier vote. Perhaps, being human, he sought peace in the family and joined the majority or simply changed his views.

Many years after the decision, abortion remains a contentious issue in America. There is no solution that will satisfy both sides. Justice Blackmun has been booed and picketed by anti-abortionists and threats were made against his life. Not long ago Texas passed a law banning late term abortions except to save the mother's life or health, or where a fetus was known to have a severe and irreversible abnormality. No exceptions are permitted for rape or incest. The controversy continues and has generated more correspondence with the United States Supreme Court than any other decision in its history As a result of the election of President Trump and his appointment of conservative justices many believe the United States Supreme Court will change or even eliminate the legal principals set forth in Roe. To counter this possibility some states are considering and New York has already passed legislation that would allow abortion in all trimesters until birth provided the mother obtains medical opinion that her health would be negatively effected by having a child. In the authors opinion such statutes heighten the possibility the court will give a constitutionally protected right to life to the fetus especially in the last trimester when the fetus could survive on its own should birth occur. Many states already recognize a fetus as a person in that a murderer guilty of killing a pregnant women and hence the fetus can be charged with two counts of murder one being of the fetus. Also, such a ruling would not contravene Roe since the decision left open abortion versus possible rights of the fetus in the last trimester. The issue is extremely divisive with those on both sides having strong views.

Recent legislative attempts to require parental approval before a minor can choose abortion have been defeated by pro choice supporters. The issue is affected by religious and moral beliefs and will not be easily dealt with in the foreseeable future. Meanwhile, Norma McCorvey became a spokesperson for the anti-abortionists... such is America.

Chapter 17

Bakke v. Regents of the University Of California

Allan bakke's life was described by one federal judge as "a storybook life of middleclass virtue". He was born in Minnesota in 1940. His father was a mailman and a teacher. He majored in engineering at the University of Minnesota where he earned close to a straight-A average. He served as a Marine combat officer in Viet Nam, ending his service as a captain. He had, according to a friend, "an almost religious zeal" to become a doctor. Because he had to take more courses to qualify for medical school while he worked for the NASA Ames Research Institute, he grew older and upon his second application for admission he was 32 years of age, somewhat older than the usual applicant. On his application he stated he was not economically or educationally disadvantaged, and in the racial category box he indicated he was White/Caucasian. The evidence showed that had Bakke indicated he was disadvantaged economically or educationally, his file would have taken a completely different course, but because he indicated "no" to that question, his application folder took the normal route. UC Davis had set up a separate admissions program for disadvantaged applicants from which Bakke was automatically excluded by his answer.

The Davis Medical School opened in 1968. Its first class had no black students and the faculty, becoming concerned, decided to set up a special admissions program "to compensate victims of unjust societal discrimination." The evidence showed that while 272 whites applied as "disadvantaged" between 1971 and 1974, not one was accepted under this special program. On the other hand, during the same period 26 blacks, 30 Mexican-Americans and 12 Asians were admitted pursuant to the special admissions program. The class Bakke applied for was fixed at 100 with 16 places reserved for special admissions applicants. The evidence showed the grade point averages and test score requirements for special admissions students were less onerous than for regular admissions candidates. Bakke's application was delayed because of the critical illness of his mother-in-law. Therefore, he was at the end of the application process when he was interviewed. His interviewer found him qualified for admissions and recommended he be admitted; however, he was only one vote on a five-member admissions committee. The combined evaluations gave Bakke a total rating of 468 out of a possible 500, but by that late date in the admissions process, his score fell just short of the needed 470 to occupy one of the few remaining seats. He was rejected and Bakke started a letter campaign which developed into a complaint that the program provided for "quotas, open or covert, for racial minorities." He stated that the rationale for quotas, based upon atonement for passed racial discrimination, was simply the institution of a new racial bias in favor of minorities, not just a solution. He felt the admission process was illegal and indicated he would formally challenge the quotas in the courts.

The chairman of the Admissions Committee, Dr. George Lowrey, asked one of his young assistants, Peter Storandt, to deal with Bakke. Interestingly, through correspondence and subsequent meetings, Storandt became an advocate of Bakke's and eventually was fired because he supported him. He also encouraged Bakke to "pursue your research into admissions policies based on quota-oriented minority recruiting." Storandt stated that although the admissions procedure tried to avoid the overtones of quotas, the fact remained that it had that effect. Although Storandt subsequently took the position he did not encourage but merely suggested Bakke bring suit, it was clear encouragement since Storandt was an admissions official.

At Storandt's suggestion, Bakke also applied for admission to the subsequent year's class. However, this time Dr. Lowrey himself interviewed Bakke and reduced his scores below that required for acceptance. It was undisputed that the interview discussion with Lowrey was centered in large part upon Bakke's opposition to the special admissions program. Justice Mosk, of the California Supreme Court noted that over half the interview by Dr. Lowrey related to the admissions program rather than Bakke's potential ability to be a medical doctor. At the same time Bakke was considering suit, there was a similar case, known as De Funis, pending against the University of Washington Law School. It was well known in educational circles the issue of race-based quotas would be decided in the courts. After Bakke's second rejection, he filed a complaint with the San Francisco Office of the Department of Health, Education and Welfare, charging U.C. Davis with racial discrimination because it had adopted "a 16% racial quota." That complaint went nowhere but it satisfied the requirement he pursue his administrative remedies before filing suit. Bakke hired San Francisco attorney Reynold H. Colvin who advised that since the DeFunis case would probably establish the law, they should wait to bring an action until that matter was decided. However, the Appellate Court sidestepped the issue in DeFunis (DeFunis v. Odegaard), therefore Colvin filed suit on behalf of Bakke in the California Superior Court of Yolo County, the location of U.C. Davis. The issue of affirmative action versus reverse discrimination was joined. This case evolved from the 1954 United States Supreme Court decision of <u>Brown v. Board of Education</u>. In that case, Chief Justice Earl Warren stated, "I don't see how in this day and age we can set any group apart from the rest and say that they are not entitled to exactly the same treatment as all others. To do so would be contrary to the 13th 14th and 15th Amendments. They were intended to make the slaves equal with all others. Personally, I can't see how today we can justify segregation based solely on race." The Supreme Court in <u>Brown</u> ruled school segregation invalid.

Many feel the presence of true equality between the races depends upon not only the absence of disabilities but also the presence of abilities. Hence, it follows that there is a social duty to make compensation for the inequalities under which racial minorities have to live. Affirmative action grew out of President Kennedy's 1961 order that government contractors had to recruit minorities and encourage their promotion. The Civil Rights Act of 1964, signed into law by President Johnson, strengthened affirmative action programs. In 1965, he stated, "You do not take a person who, for years has been hobbled by change and liberate him, bring him up to the starting line of a race and then say, 'You are free to compete with all the others,' and still justly believe that you have been completely fair."

He believed the nation needed to move beyond the point where equality was a right or theory to a position where equality was in fact a reality. Was the application process at Davis aimed at admitting certain students or excluding others? Where does one place the emphasis?

The first trial was before a retired judge from Sonoma County sitting by assignment in Yolo County because its two judges disqualified themselves based upon some unspecified relationship with the University. The judge, Leslie Manker, a U.C. Berkeley graduate, had been appointed to the Superior Court of Sonoma County by Governor Pat Brown in

1964. At the time of the trial in 1970 he was 67 years old and had been retired for five years. He was sitting in Yolo County upon assignment of the Judicial Council. The Judge came into the case thinking it would be the usual run-of-the-mill matter and attorney Colvin recalled, "From the look on his face, I think he felt he had been done in." Since the facts were virtually undisputed and the only witness was Dr. Lowrey, the case was heard in a brief time. Colvin argued simply, "Equal protection means nondiscrimination and Bakke's exclusion was a result of racial classification. Hence, he was the victim of racial discrimination." He had a rather straightforward argument in that if "the Constitution prohibits exclusion of Blacks and other minorities on racial grounds it cannot permit the exclusion of Whites on racial grounds." Therefore, it follows the admission policy violated Bakke's 14th Amendment right to equal protection of the law. The University was represented by its general counsel, Donald L. Reidhaar, who had previously advised University of California President Charles Hitch that preferences based upon race violated the U.S. Constitution. Despite this, he did his best to defend his client and support the Davis program. The Civil Rights Act of 1964 states:

> "No person in the United States shall, on the grounds of race, color or national origin, be excluded from participation in, be denied the benefits of, or be subjected to discrimination under any program or activity receiving federal or financial assistance."

Reidhaar argued the law should be interpreted to permit giving special consideration to minority group members in admissions for the purpose of increasing their participation in educational programs. He took the position that the power of the State was being used affirmatively to combat discrimination and make the promise of the 14th Amendment a reality.

In late 1974, Judge Manker issued a Notice of Intended Decision wherein he stated the admissions program violated the law, but Bakke himself had not proven he should have been admitted since Dr. Lowrey's testimony made it clear there was wide discretion in the admissions process. The Court refused to issue an order directing Davis to admit Bakke; however, it did grant his request for an injunction prohibiting U.C. Davis from the consideration of race in its admission process. His judgment declared the special admissions program at the University of California Davis Medical School violated the 14th Amendment to the United States Constitution, Article I, Section 21 of the California Constitution and the Federal Civil Rights Act of 1964. The Judge's decision was not agreeable to either the plaintiff or defendant and although an appeal would normally go to the California Court ofAppeals, in this case, the California Supreme Court issued an order accepting the appeal directly. Hence, it arrived at that Court rather quickly.

The argument was heard on March 18, 1976 with Chief Justice Donald Wright leading off the questioning. It was reported that attorney Reidhaar was much more relaxed than Colvin. However, Colvin had Justice Mosk on his side. That became clear when Justice Mosk stated, "Indeed about 20 to 30 points better qualified than the 16 that were given preferential treatment." He said this in response to Reidhaar's statement that Mr. Bakke was present in court and that there was never any suggestion he was not qualified to undertake medical study. In rebuttal to Justice Mosk's statement, Reidhaar stated, "If one looks simply to a comparison of paper records." In other words, Reidhaar conceded that not only was Bakke qualified but that he was more qualified "on paper" than the 16 admitted under the quota. It must be noted that often cases turn on which party has the burden of proof. Colvin argued that once he proved that racial discrimination occurred, the burden to rebut shifted to the opponent. This became crucial in hearings before the U.S. Supreme Court which accepted Colvin's position that racial discrimination was proved, hence, the University had the burden to prove Bakke should be excluded on some acceptable basis.

The California Supreme Court decision was issued on September 16, 1976 and was a complete victory for Bakke. The majority opinion was written by Justice Mosk who was joined by all the other justices except Justice Tobriner who wrote a strong dissent. Justice Tobriner was, along with Justice Mosk, considered the most liberal member of the California Supreme Court hence his opposition was not a surprise to anyone. The decision pointed out the special admissions program denied admission to white applicants solely because of race. Although a compelling state interest was demonstrated, there must be a reasonable way to achieve the goals other than a program that provides some individuals a higher degree of protection against unequal treatment than others. On the other hand, Justice Tobriner argued that the Court had always been in the forefront of protecting the rights of minorities and that U.C. Davis should not be precluded from pursuing programs to provide for effective integration at the school. However, Bakke carried the day by proving a race-based quota was used.

To appeal or not to appeal became the issue for the Regents of the University of California. Since all race-based admissions programs were barred, they chose to appeal and the title of the case changed to Regents of the University of California v. Bakke. Now the Regents had the burden of proof as the appellant.

On February 18, 1977, the United States Supreme Court voted to grant certiorari, a writ requesting the Court hear the case. Generally, each justice assigns one or more clerks to prepare a draft opinion based upon input from the justice. Eventually, the justice prepares a memorandum of his position which is circulated to the other justices. After a conference, the Chief Justice then appoints one of the justices in the majority of whatever issue is under review to write the opinion. In the <u>Bakke</u> case, the opinion was assigned by Chief Justice Warren E. Burger to Justice Lewis F. Powell, Jr. He found the special admissions program was undeniably a classification based on race and ethnic background. Citing the 14th Amendment: "'No state shall deny to any person within its jurisdiction equal protection of the law," he wrote the guaranty of equal protection is a personal right applied to all citizens of the state. He further stated, "If both are not entitled to the same protection, then it is not equal."

Legal restrictions curtailing the rights of a single racial group are immediately suspect as was pointed out in the cases involving the incarceration of Japanese Americans during World War II, It is not that any such restrictions are unconstitutional; however, they are subject to close scrutiny. He found racial and ethnic distinctions of any sort inherently suspect and must call for the most critical judicial examination. He argued that the University's position that discrimination against members of the white majority cannot be suspect was incorrect. He stated the concepts of majority and minority necessarily reflect temporary judgments and political arrangements. The white majority itself is necessarily composed of various minority groups, each of which can lay claim to a list of prior discrimination at the hands of the state and private individuals. If these classifications based on race and ethnicity were broken down, the present arguable majority may in actuality end up being a new minority of White Anglo-Saxon Protestants. The courts cannot be asked to evaluate the extent of the prejudice and consequent harm suffered by various minority groups. Preferential programs are not supported in the Constitution. Some individuals cannot be asked to suffer impermissible burdens for the greater good of other ethnic groups. Preferential programs may only reinforce common stereotypes, holding that certain groups are unable to achieve success without special protection based on a factor having no relationship to actual individual worth. The Constitution does not provide for innocent persons bearing the burden of redressing grievances not of their making.

Justice Powell went on to use an amicus curia brief filed by Harvard with the support of Columbia, the University of Pennsylvania and Stanford. These briefs argued that awareness of disadvantaged economic, racial and ethnic groups was appropriate for consideration by colleges and universities that wish to have their student bodies represent a cross section of America, just as geographical awareness is appropriate. However, there is a difference between admissions programs that include this awareness and quotas based on the aforementioned factors.

Chief Justice Warren E. Berger found the objectives of the University of California laudable but their methods extreme. He found the rigidly cast admissions program impermissible and could not believe the Regents pursued the least offensive or intrusive method of promoting an important state interest. Justice William H. Rehnquist later a Chief Justice of the U.S. Supreme Court found in a memorandum dated November 10, 1977, that the University's affirmative action program was as difficult to sustain constitutionally as one conceivably could be. He distinguished between cases of "disparate impact" (as between minority groups and majority groups) and this case which was one of race-based quotas. Applying this strict scrutiny standard and putting the burden on the University of California, Justice Rehnquist joined Justice Powell in the majority.

Justice Harry A. Blackmun took the <u>Bakke</u> case to heart. In fact he held off preparing his memorandum and only submitted it after being pressed by the Chief Justice. It is dated May 1, 1978, and he voted to reverse based upon his strong feeling that although he wished "affirmative action" programs were unnecessary and a relic of the past, in reality he believed they were necessary to overcome past discrimination. He was clearly bothered by the fact that only 2% of all physicians and attorneys in the United States were members of minority groups and that just about all black doctors came from just two schools. He pointed out that universities for years conceded preferences based upon athletic skill, to the children of alumni, to the affluent who bestowed endowments on institutions or to those having connections with celebrities. He states no one seems to be concerned about those practices and believes programs of admissions should be best left to academians and administrators. He felt an admissions policy that had an awareness of race as an element was logical, realistic and would help achieve societal goals he found laudable. He felt Congress when passing Title VI (Civil Rights Act of 1964) was concerned with private constitutional race criteria, not with the use of race as an appropriate remedial feature. He felt there was no independent cause of action under Title VI but was willing to assume that a private cause of action does exist and that Bakke had standing to bring the action. He found governmental preferences were common, i.e., veterans' preferences, aid to handicapped programs, progressive income tax, Indian programs and in the educational field, consideration of geography, and other factors. He felt the Davis program was benign and did not carry a stigma.

Finally, after a period of over two months, sometimes known as the "waiting for Harry" period, the position of the Court became clear. Chief Justice Warren Berger, Justices Stewart, Rehnquist and Stevens wanted to affirm the judgment for Bakke based on the 1964 Civil Rights Act. On the other side were Justices Brennan, White and Marshall. Now they were joined by Justice Blackmun. Therefore, it was

4 to 4. Justice Powell was the deciding vote and he took an interesting position in that while he agreed with Bakke that the special admissions program was unlawful, he also agreed with the Brennan four that the portion of the judgment enjoining any consideration of race in the admissions process should be reversed.

The Justices had patiently waited for Blackmun to adopt his position. He had the reputation of being somewhat indecisive and slow. Actually, Blackmun had become annoyed at Justice Brennan holding out on a vote in another case and made it clear that he would not vote in Bakke until Brennan voted in a case known as Baldwin thus we have a glimpse of inner Supreme Court politics.

Justice Thurgood Marshall issued what became known as "the cruelest irony" memorandum. He looked at the problem fairly objectively as being one admitting certain students, or on the other hand, excluding others. He wanted to pursue a "color blindness" view but that would ignore his belief that the economic disparity between the races was increasing. He stated:

> "The dream ofAmerica as the melting pot has not been realized by negroes—either the negro did not get into the pot, or he did not get melted down. Instead, all statistics document the differences between white and black America brought about by centuries of slavery, with the approval of this Court, which permitted negroes to be treated specially."

On Wednesday, June 27, 1978, the Supreme Court issued its decision. Justice Powell delivered the judgment of the Court in No. 76-811, Regents of the University of California v. Bakke. Since the case had resulted in nationwide publicity, Justice Powell stated the facts were too well known to require restatement. He pointed out the two central questions were: (1) Is the Medical School special admissions program unlawful under the Constitution or the Civil Rights Act of 1964, i.e., the Bakke admission question; and (2) whether it is ever permissible to consider race as a factor relevant to the admission of applicants to a university. He referred to this question generally as whether race may be considered. He answered the second question first. He joined Justices Brennan, White, Marshall and Blackman in holding race may properly be considered but he refused to join them in holding the Davis Medical School admissions programs was valid. Therefore, he joined Chief Justice Burger, Justice Stevens, Justice Stewart and Justice Rehnquist in finding Title VI (the Civil Rights Act of 1964) controls and that Bakke was excluded in violation of that statute; hence, the majority of the Court found that Bakke must be admitted to the Medical School.

The decision referenced the Harvard admission program as an example of how race may properly be taken into account. Under that program, "race is considered in a flexible program designed to achieve diversity, but it is only one factor—weighed competitively, against a number of other factors being relevant." He went on to state it was "a flexible, competitive admissions program in which race may be considered.. used in many of our finest universities and colleges." He found the Davis program to be arbitrary in that it foreclosed competition solely on the basis of race or ethnic origin and was not necessary to attain reasonable educational diversity. Therefore, the program violated the Equal Protection Clause of the United States Constitution.

Interestingly, justices usually read summaries of their views when decisions are made and Justice Brennan points out that "Five of us, a court majority, reversed the judgment of the California Supreme Court insofar as it prohibits Davis from establishing race-conscious admissions programs in the future. Thus, the central meaning of today's opinion is this: Government may take race into account when it acts not to demean or insult any racial group, but to remedy disadvantages cast on minorities by past racial prejudice, at least when appropriate findings have been made by judicial, legislative or administrative bodies with competence to act in this area." In summary, the United States Supreme Court found race-based quotas in education violates the 14th Amendment to the United States Constitution Equal Protection Clause and the 1964 Civil Rights Act. However, it also held race can be taken into consideration as part of a process in the admissions criteria for students seeking admission to schools. This issue was raised again by members of the Board of Regents of the University of California and the academic leadership of that university. Also, the United States Supreme Court again addressed the issue. Its ruling in the two University of Michigan cases of Gratz v. Bollinger and Grutter v. Bollinger followed the thinking of Justice Powell in this case. On the other hand, California Proposition 209 precludes race being considered in any manner for admission. Perhaps Justice Blackman saw the future when he stated these decisions should be best dealt with by academians and administrators who have to find their way through the various policies.

CHAPTER 18

THE IMPEACHMENT AND TRIAL OF ANDREW JOHNSON

DID THE PRESIDENT, OR as some claimed Acting President and Vice-President Andrew Johnson, while fulfilling the duties of President, engage in corrupt acts that constituted abuse of power including improper use of the presidential veto power to defeat the will of the people, interfere with elections, and more specifically did he violate the Tenure of Office Act by attempting to discharge his Secretary of War, Edwin Stanton, who was also a member of the Presidential cabinet?

Notwithstanding the fact he was a lifelong Democrat and slaveholder, Andrew Johnson, a member of the House of Representatives from Tennessee, was chosen to serve as the vice presidential candidate on the 1864 Republican ticket led by Abraham Lincoln. It was obvious he was chosen in an effort to cater to northern war advocates and because he alone of the members of Congress from the south opposed succession and vehemently argued against it. He was considered a turncoat by southern legislators and this would play a part in his ultimate impeachment and trial. As the Civil War came to a conclusion, a number of border states were quickly readmitted to the union, and were therefore able to send representatives to Congress to represent their interests. An example of the unusual circumstance is reflected by the situation in the State of Virginia. Since the area now known as West Virginia was pro-union, it was allowed to send new senators to Congress while Virginia itself also had two senators in place. At the same time, just before the war ended, Virginia had two senators representing its interest in the Confederate Legislature in Richmond, Virginia. Other border states that quickly obtained representation were Tennessee, Louisiana and Arkansas.

In the 39th Congress, which sat from December 1865 through 1866, 25 non-seceding states were represented by 50 senators, 39 Republicans and 11 Democrats. There were 184 representatives in the House, 141 Republicans and 43 Democrats. Should the 11 states which had to be "reconstructed" send representatives to Congress, it would add 22 senators and 58 representatives just about all of whom would be Democrats. That would result in the Republican majority being reduced from 28 to 6 in the Senate and in the House from 98 to 40. Four Democratic senators actually supported Lincoln's policies and were swing votes. The Republicans were concerned new members would reduce their majority and make the south more powerful hence their opposition to the reconstruction plan set out by President Lincoln and Vice-President Johnson. The opposition was led by Senator Thaddeus Stevens, an arch abolitionist, whose lands were damaged by Lee's excursions into the north. He wanted to confiscate southern lands and strongly believed Congress rather than the executive branch of government should oversee reconstruction.

Stevens set up a committee of six senators and nine representatives to decide on the admission of members from the seceded states. Among the many issues to be dealt with were the parameters of readmission and negro suffrage.

During this time Congress was working on the passage of the Fourteenth Amendment which would reduce representation of states that withheld the right to vote from negroes (Fourteenth Amendment, Section Two). Fearing an escalation of violence, President Johnson opposed the bill and its supporters could not override his veto by a two-thirds vote. Congress passed a law giving negroes in the District of Columbia the right to vote and Johnson vetoed the bill again fearing violence.

Republicans moved against Johnson by admitting territories such as Nebraska and Colorado in an effort to add senators to their majority. They then moved to politically decapitate the President and control reconstruction.

During this tumultuous time, Congress passed the Tenure of Office Act which required the consent of the Senate to remove all government officials whose appointment required the consent of the Senate. This squarely engaged both sides and put into controversy their respective legal powers. Initially, the House of Representatives excepted cabinet members, however, when the bill went to Senate and then a conference committee, the exception was removed. The bill was passed and the President vetoed it. The bill was then passed by a two-thirds vote overcoming the veto. The executive branch of government felt the law was unconstitutional.

The Reconstruction Act dealt with the ten states not yet readmitted as of 1867. It divided the states into five military districts as follows: First — Virginia; Second — North and South Carolina; Third — Georgia, Alabama and Florida; Fourth — Mississippi and Arkansas; Fifth — Louisiana and Texas. The law provided a general officer would command each district basically as an absolute monarch. It also provided that all orders to them had to pass through the General In Chief who at that time was Ulysses S. Grant, hence interfering in the President's powers as Commander and Chief. Edwin M. Stanton was Secretary of War and although he appeared to cooperate with the President he was in league with Steven's committee. Also, rumors were circulated during the May 1867 trial of Jefferson Davis that Johnson had been in conspiracy with Davis to assassinate President Lincoln. An investigation was launched but no facts were developed to prove the theory.

When Johnson learned Stanton was working with his opponents in Congress and that he felt totally protected by the Tenure of Office Act, Johnson decided to remove him and asked General Grant to provide his advice. Grant sided with the Tenure of Office Act supporters and refused to become involved. President Johnson then asked General Sheridan if he would act as Secretary of War and remove Stanton. Sheridan declined because he did not want to engage in politics and believed replacing Stanton would violate the law. Meanwhile, Stanton refused Johnson's request for his resignation. Finally, Grant agreed to act as Interim Secretary of War although again Stanton refused to leave office. Johnson managed to replace all the commanding generals appointed by Stanton to control the five military districts. The policy that the military was subservient to civil power was reinforced.

At the same time Congress passed the Fourteenth Amendment and it was quickly ratified by two-thirds of the states. Its purpose was to control the ten states that were to be readmitted. Elections in the northern states in 1867 indicated popular opinion was against the Republicans' reconstruction policies. In New York, New Jersey, Maine, California, Ohio and Pennsylvania, numerous Democrats were elected. Many were against negro suffrage.

The House of Representatives attempted to impeach President Johnson because of his dismissal of Stanton but failed 108 to 57. The allegations were very general and were based more on what congressmen thought Johnson would do in the future rather than past events. Although 99 witnesses were called, no real crime was developed. There was much testimony regarding malfeasance, usurption of power, abuse of the pardoning power and returning confiscated property to secessionists. He was also charged with using the veto power to defeat the will of the people (as represented by Congress).

The real issues in this first impeachment attempt were the return of property and pardons. Also the executive branch was not requiring the oath of allegiance known as the Test Oath which was demanded by Congress.

Shortly after the failed impeachment vote, Johnson notified Congress of his reasons for removing Stanton. A commission was formed and it decided Stanton should be returned to office. General Grant, not wanting to be held in violation of the Tenure Act, left the office and Stanton returned. Apparently, at that time, no one in power felt it necessary to respect the President's authority. It was said he obtained the office while he was drunk and was only temporarily holding the office not having been elected President. Of course the unwelcome Stanton stopped attending cabinet meetings and he never again entered the White House.

A series of letters back and forth between Johnson, Grant and Stanton ensued. These letters were subsequently used as evidence to prove Johnson's violation of the Tenure Act. The President convinced General Lorenzo Thomas, the hero of the Battle of Chickamauga, to act as Interim Secretary of War. General Thomas tried to evict Stanton who refused, and Stanton, going to the courts, obtained a warrant from Justice Cartter of the Federal District Court for the arrest of Thomas. The U.S. Marshal tracked him down, arrested him and then he was released on bail. The President was satisfied that finally the issue would be decided in the courts so he turned his attention to the impeachment allegations he knew were again being prepared. The Senate assumed a conviction would result because the letters were evidence of a violation of the Tenure Act. They assumed the courts could not stop them and then

Vice-President Ben Wade would become President in the near future. Rumors were circulated that Johnson wanted control of the Army to ensure his election as President in the 1867 Presidential election.

The Sixth Section of the Tenure Act states "Every removal..." contrary to the act was a high misdemeanor punishable by a fine of up to $10,000 and five years in prison (that punishment would make it a felony in present day law). Another provision of the act made it a violation to issue any letter of authority contrary to the act. President Johnson had issued such letters to Generals Grant and Thomas.

Ironically, it was pointed out Stanton still occupied the office and Johnson had simply issued an order to General Thomas which he was entitled to do as Commander and Chief. How could it be said that Stanton was removed? It was argued it was an attempt but the act does not punish attempts. Quickly the main argument was addressed whether or not Stanton was protected by the act.

The Tenure Act also provided that a month after the President's term expired, those appointed as cabinet members subsequently served at the sufferance of the next President. The act only protected appointees from being removed by the appointing President without the consent of the Senate. In response, the argument was made Lincoln's term was four years and Johnson was simply serving that term. Meanwhile General Thomas, through his lawyer, filed a writ of habeas corpus. Judge Cartter pointed out Thomas was not in custody so there was no need for the writ, however Thomas' attorney made it clear that they wanted to appeal a ruling denying the writ to the U.S. Supreme Court. The Judge, seeing where this was going, decided to simply discharge Thomas making the issue moot and that in fact was the end of the case against the General.

The impeachment in the House of Representatives was pressed by Congressman and former Civil War General Benjamin Butler who even during the war was known as a political general. He had served in

Louisiana and then commanded the Army of the James as it approached Richmond. He failed in his objectives and although he kept his political clout was not considered much of a general.

Was the appointment of a cabinet officer an executive act or a legislative act? There were only three possibilities regarding removal. The first was it was in the power of the President alone to do so, the second was it was in the power of both the President and the Senate, and the third was the Constitution was silent on the point and that the Legislature could pass legislation to deal with the matter. In response, the argument was made it takes three acts for a cabinet member to be appointed. The first was the nomination by the President, the second the consent of the Senate, and third the President had to issue a commission. Since the Senate could affirm a nomination but the President then not execute the commission, it was argued the President had the final power and that the Senate's consent was not the final act required for an appointment hence a cabinet member was in fact an executive appointment.

Eleven articles of impeachment passed the House, the first ten dealt with specific speeches or letters. It was the 11th that specifically charged the violation of the Tenure of Office Act. Congressman Benjamin Butler led the House managers who brought the case to the Senate. The trial was presided over by Supreme Court Chief Justice Chase. General Thomas, General Sherman and many others testified. Evidence was generally admitted if it had any reasonable relationship to the matters at hand. The Senate often overrode Chief Justice Chase's rulings on evidence and let just about all evidence offered into the hearings.

Finally, on Saturday, May 16, 1868, Chief Justice Chase called the High Court of Impeachment to order. All 54 senators were present except Grimes who was ill. However he subsequently appeared in the chamber. A motion was made that the vote be taken on the 11th article of impeachment first since that would indicate which way the senate was leaning. The role was called and when it reached 25 votes for impeachment with another 10 known to support it, it became obvious that there were 35 votes for impeachment. Senator Ross of Kansas who had kept his own counsel elected to vote not guilty and the chamber went silent. The final vote was 35 to convict and 19 to acquit-one less than the required two-thirds (36) necessary for a conviction.

A motion was made to continue the matter to a later date and when the vote was finally held it was the same for all ten articles. Some writers argue that never again would a president be impeached for political reasons. It was pointed out the offense must clearly be a high crime or misdemeanor to obtain a conviction.

At the Democratic Convention in 1868, Johnson was not a candidate. His party disavowed him and of course the Republicans wanted nothing to do with a democrat. Just before leaving office Johnson pardoned all those involved in the rebellion. When questioned regarding his authority to do so, he quoted Section 2 of Article 2 of the United States Constitution. He also referred to similar acts in the past performed by numerous presidents including Washington, Adams and Jefferson.

The sole accomplishment of the Congress that year was to pass the Fifteenth Amendment giving negroes the right to vote. Attempts to repeal portions of the Tenure Act were successful and little by little it was amended until finally what was left was declared unconstitutional by the United States Supreme Court in 1926.

How does the impeachment and trial of Andrew Johnson compare with that of William Clinton? In the case of Johnson, the impeachment relied heavily on the alleged violation of an unconstitutional law. In the case of William Clinton, the underlying violation of law was perjury, historically a felony. What do the words "high crimes and misdemeanors" really mean? A history of the words from the constitutional convention, as related by Madison, points out that the original wording was "formal or corrupt conduct" or "for malpractice or neglect of duty".

Subsequently the wording was modified so as to state "for treason, bribery, or corruption," and finally the words were reduced to "treason and bribery" alone. Colonel Mason again moved to add the words "maladministration" and Madison objected that the terms were so vague that they would be the equivalent of granting the president tenure at the pleasure of the Senate. Mason withdrew the word and substituted "other high crimes and misdemeanors against the state" which was finally agreed to with the removal of the words "against the state." It is argued that because of this history, the violation must be of a high crime or high misdemeanor of the type known in common law as being on a par with treason or bribery. In the case of Johnson, it was violation of a law which he felt was unconstitutional, and in the case of Clinton, it was violation of a law which is generally considered a felony but which also in some circumstances can be a misdemeanor. It was not, even if it were true, in a matter that involved his office or specific governmental interest.

However, when removing the words "against the state" were the framers of the Constitution simply looking at those words as being superfluous or did they intend to include crimes that were not necessarily against specific governmental interests? The removal of the words "against the state," was done to remove surplusage. Because impeachment is a political remedy, one can argue the charges should have some nexus or connection with the office. Other types of illegalities can be criminally prosecuted once the President leaves office.

Chapter 19

Impeachment and Trial of William Jefferson Clinton

Was president of the United States William Jefferson Clinton guilty of a high crime or high misdemeanor so as to warrant impeachment, conviction, and removal from office pursuant to Article II, Section 4 of the Constitution of the United States? More specifically, did President William J. Clinton engage in immoral sexual acts with a White House intern named Monica Lewinsky on a number of occasions beginning at a time when government employees were furloughed because of budget failure. The only staff in the White House allowed to function were unpaid volunteer interns. One of those volunteers was Lewinsky. Was it the crisis mode in Washington or simply lust that caused Bill Clinton to engage in reckless acts that jeopardized his presidency and created a constitutional crisis in our government? Perhaps it was both. He has stated he did it because he could and admits he was morally corrupt. One could reasonably wish he had made the admission earlier and saved himself, his family and the country from the ensuing ordeal.

However, he was not impeached and tried for these acts which although "un-presidential" and morally questionable were not illegal.

He committed these acts at a time when he was subject to being deposed under oath in two matters. The first was a sexual harassment law suit brought by Paula Jones. The second matter was the President's testimony before a grand jury empaneled by Special Prosecutor Ken Starr.

Monica Lewinsky, a young woman in her early 20's, was expected by the President to stay silent regarding their relationship and one must also question his judgment in that regard. She told her friend, Linda Tripp, of her secret relationship and the "friend" taped the conversation. Monica also kept a blue dress with semen on it for a long period of time and, again, one must ask why she never had it cleaned. Between December 19, 1997 and August 17, 1998, the President, unaware of the tape or dress, chose on six different occasions to be less than fully truthful regarding the matter and on two of those occasions he was under oath.

When Linda Tripp first leaked the story and it gained widespread circulation, Clinton and his lawyer, William Bennett, decided to obtain an affidavit from Monica Lewinsky wherein she would deny the relationship. At approximately 2:00 a.m. on the morning of December 17, 1997, the President called Ms. Lewinsky and they discussed the contents of the affidavit. Since she agreed to sign the document, the President felt safe in denying the relationship. One must question his lawyer's strategy, relying on the viability of an affidavit from a young woman, without making it clear to the President that her unusual and well known access to the Oval Office may well result in her credibility being attacked along with his.

On December 23, 1997, the President signed, under oath, written interrogatories (questions under oath) wherein he denied having had sexual relations with any federal employees while he was President of the United States. Being a wordsmith the President could argue, as an intern, she was not a federal employee since she was unpaid and that the acts they engaged in were not sexual relations. Regardless of interpretation, his intent was to deceive and he continued on that course with the American public for a long time. Does this course of action give rise to an impeachable offense?

What is perjury? Simply put, it is lying under oath. The oath creates a duty to tell the truth and a violation of the oath is perjury. Unfortunately, it is not an uncommon crime and it is rarely prosecuted. Successful prosecution requires the testimony to be clearly a lie and if the defendant has any opportunity to argue the meaning of words, a perjury conviction may not result. Bill Clinton was a lawyer and knew these arguments. No doubt anticipating he would be asked if he had intercourse, he avoided having to answer in the affirmative by engaging in other sexual acts which would be difficult for a lawyer taking his testimony to specifically question him about. The whole issue of perjury was dominated by lawyers. Not only was Clinton a lawyer but he was advised by at least two other lawyers. There were lawyers taking his deposition and helping him answer interrogatories and there were a great number of lawyers in the Congress that impeached, tried and failed to convict him. One could look at this sordid mess and describe it as a "lawyers' game," but that would be unfair, since in reality it was the President of the United States who engaged in deception, and it's possible his own lawyers did not want to know the truth. Had they known the truth, they certainly would have or should have advised him to pursue a different course than he chose. We are a forgiving people. His lawyers should have helped him to understand that fact.

The formal articles of impeachment passed by the House of Representatives set forth four charges: (1) providing false and misleading testimony to the grand jury on August 17, 1998; (2) providing false and misleading testimony in the Paula Jones sexual harassment lawsuit; (3) obstructing justice in the Jones case; and (4) making false and misleading statements to Congress. The President was not impeached on Articles 2 and 4. Articles 1 and 3 were sent to the Senate for trial. These were two very specific acts, perjury before a grand jury and obstruction of justice in the Jones case. In the House of Representatives, the vote on Article 1, perjury, was 228 for impeachment and 206 against. On Article 3, obstruction of justice, the vote was 221 for 212 against.

Were the articles of impeachment appropriate? Did William Jefferson Clinton commit a high crime or high misdemeanor? Generally, perjury is considered a felony which is a high crime. Occasionally it is charged as a misdemeanor, or as a result of a misdemeanor sentence being imposed, a felony can be reduced to a misdemeanor. However, there is no support for the idea that perjury is not at the very least a high misdemeanor. Therefore, even though the impeachment and trial process is political in nature, it must be based on the commission of a crime. Clinton's sexual encounters with Monica Lewinsky were not illegal and he could not have been impeached for those acts. However, his subterfuge created a situation wherein he arguably violated the law and committed an impeachable offense.

Since 1868 when Andrew Johnson was impeached and tried for violating the Tenure of Office Act for firing Secretary of War Edwin Stanton, Congress has been careful to avoid creating a constitutional crisis by utilizing this political tool to unseat a president. It is purely political since the penalty is removal from office and only thereafter can the official still be charged for the commission of crimes in a court of law. Johnson only escaped being convicted by one vote in the Senate, hence the gravity of the procedure was recognized and therefore has not been seriously pursued without due deliberation. Some question whether Clinton should have been impeached feeling it was entirely political. However, it is in fact a political remedy, albeit a serious one, that must be utilized properly.

Whereas President Johnson, after the Civil War, felt the Tenure of Office Act was unconstitutional and refused to follow it (it was in fact declared unconstitutional by the United States Supreme Court in <u>Myers v. United States</u> in 1926). President Clinton had no such argument to support his alleged violation of perjury and obstruction laws. He initially denied and then admitted his sexual encounters with Monica Lewinsky and at the same time denied he had committed perjury. The real issue in the minds of many was should Clinton be removed from office for lying to cover up an immoral and adulterous act. Many did not look directly at the issue of whether or not he committed a serious crime while pursuing his deceptive course of action. Many who did consider it a crime simply decided it was not serious enough to remove a president from office and that is the political nature of impeachment and trial in the Senate. The Senate should try to reflect the will of the electorate and in this case probably accomplished that goal. On the other hand, the Senate did not want to let him off completely. Approximately 38 Democrats supported a resolution by Senator Dianne Feinstein to censure the President. However, it was not joined by most Republicans because they wanted a conviction. Since conviction required a two-thirds vote of the Senate, which meant over 10 Democrats would have to side with Republicans to vote for conviction, it was probably not possible to convict Clinton of Articles 1 or 3. Why didn't the Republicans accept censure? The answer is obviously political and that again highlights the nature of the process.

Clinton's defense in the Senate argued that the framers of the Constitution only intended impeachment and removal from office for crimes against our system of government. They argued that since the framers specifically made treason, bribery or corruption impeachable offenses, they were only concerned about crimes against the state. Hence they argued, the words "other high crimes and misdemeanors 'were intended to mean only those against the state. The defense denied the words encompassed all criminal law. Reference the Impeachment and Trial of Andrew Johnson for a more detailed analysis of what the framers of the Constitution intended. History has not yet judged Bill Clinton and/or his presidency. His sexual encounters with a White House intern will simply be called an improper relationship. It will be clear he lied but not about something most people believe is very important. His impeachment and trial will be viewed as being only political and, in fact, that is true.

Has the resignation of President Richard Nixon, the impeachment and trial of William Clinton and the controversies surrounding the Trump presidency cheapened the presidency? Have we, by becoming a polarized society, greatly affected by 24 hours a day of media bombardment, become so cynical that we are more interested in destroying than creating; tearing down rather than building, and in general being willing pawns in the great manipulation of our ideals such as family, religion, law and freedom?

Unfortunately, our history indicates the public reacts to extremes and so extremes are our topics of discussion. More often now than before, the courts are becoming the arbiter of not only our laws but our social policies. Are the three branches of our government really doing their jobs? Probably not! Are we allowing them to do so? Probably not!

Do we really want them to do so? Yes, but for that to occur, the great majority in the middle must enter and moderate the conversation.

Acknowledgment

I UNDERTOOK THIS WORK because it combines my interest in history, the law and good stories. It would not have been possible without the sage guidance and encouragement from my wife of over 56 years, Sue Lanahan, and my daughter, Karen Frank.

I wish to thank all my students at Sonoma State University, Empire Law School and San Francisco Law school for their enthusiasm and encouragement.

Daniel J. Lanahan
Puerto Vallarta
March 2019

WORKS CONSULTED

Adler, Renata. Reckless Disregard: Westmoreland v CBS et al.; Sharon v. Time. New York: Alfred A. Knopf, 1986.

Carter, Dan T. Scottsboro: A Tragedy of the American South. Baton Rouge: Louisiana State University Press, 1969.

Cornell, Julien. The Trial of Ezra Pound: A Documented Account of the Treason Case by the Defendant's Lawyer. New York: The John Day Company, 1966.

Dershowitz, Alan. The Case Against Impeaching Trump. Skyhorse Publishing, Inc. 2018

Dewitt, David Miller. The Impeachment and Trial of Andrew Johnson, Seventeenth President of the United States: A History. New York: The Macmillan Company, 1903.

Dower, John W. Embracing Defeat: Japan in the Wake of World War II. New York: WY. Norton and Company / The New Press, 1999.

Ellsberg, Daniel. Secrets: A Memoir of Vietnam and the Pentagon Papers. New York: Viking, 2002.

Epstein, Jason. <u>The Great Conspiracy Trial: An Essay on Law Liberty and the Constitution</u>. New York: Random House, 1970.

Faux, Marian. <u>Roe v. Wade: The Untold Story of the Landmark Supreme Court Decision That Made Abortion Legal</u>. New York: Macmillan Publishing Company, 1988.

Fraenkel, Osmond K. <u>The Sacco-Vanzetti Case</u>. New York: Alfred A. Knopf Inc. 1931.

<u>The Impeachment and Trial of President Clinton: The Official Transcripts from The House Judiciary Committee Hearings to the Senate Trial</u>. Intro. Michael R. Beschloss. Ed. Merrill McLoughlin. New York: Times Books Random House, 1999.

Kaplan, John and Waltz, Jon R. <u>The Trial of Jack Ruby</u>. New York: The Macmillan Company, 1965.

Kessler, Ronald. <u>The Bureau: The Secret History of the FBI</u>. New York: St Martin's Press, 2002.

McKernan, Maureen. <u>The Amazing Crime and Trial of Leopold and Loeb</u>. Chicago: The Plymouth Court Press, 1924.

Pearson, Edmund. <u>Trial of Lizzie Borden: Edited, with a History of the Case</u>. Garden City, New York: Doubleday, Doran and Company, Inc., 1937.

Radosh, Ronald and Milton, Joyce. <u>The Rosenberg File: A Search for the Truth</u>. New York: Holt, Rinehart and Winston, 1983.

Schwartz, Bernard. <u>Behind Bakke: Affirmative Action and the Supreme Court</u>. New York: New York University Press, 1988.

Seidemann, Joel J. <u>In the Interest of Justice</u>. Harper Collins Publishing, 2004

Smolla, Rod. <u>Deliberate Intent: A Lawyer Tells the True Story of Murder by the Book</u>. New York: Crown Publishers, 1999.

Smolla, Rodney A. <u>Jerry Falwell v. Larry Flynt: The First Amendment on Trial</u>. New York: St Martin's Press, 1988.

Tusa, Ann and Tusa, John. <u>The Nuremberg Trial</u>. New York: Atheneum, 1986.

Westin, Alan F. and Mahoney, Barry. <u>The Trial of Martin Luther King</u>. New York: Thomas Y. Crowell Company, Inc., 1974.

<u>The World's Most Famous Trial: Tennessee Evolution Case</u>. Cincinnati, Ohio: National Book Company, 1925.

Ungar, Sanford. <u>The Paper and the Papers: An Account of the legal Battle over the Pentagon Papers</u>. New York: Columbia University Press, 1972.

All of the above mentioned works, except those by Ellsberg, Dershowitz, Dower, Kessler and Seidemann, were privately printed for the members of the Notable Trials Library, a division of Gryphon Editions

About The Author

Daniel J Lanahan was born in Brooklyn at the beginning of World War Two. After three plus years active duty in the U.S. Army and college, he worked as an insurance investigator and claims manager while attending law school. During his almost 50 years as a member of the California Bar he often pursued other interests. His entire legal career was spent at two law firms, Ropers Majeski for 26 years where he was a senior partner and Lanahan & Reilley LLP which he cofounded with Martin Reilley in 1997. Mr. Lanahan partially and then fully retired between 2006 and 2010.

He also worked as a police officer, including stints as a patrolman and legal officer for a San Francisco Bay area police department. He taught the laws of search and seizure, arrests and the use of firearms at a police academy. His published book on those subjects was utilized by law enforcement. In 1977 he and six others founded the Bay Area Bank in Redwood City and San Carlos. He served on its board and as Corporate Secretary until retiring from Banking in 1991. Bay Area Bankcorp was subsequently purchased by Wells Fargo Bank.

In the 1980's and 1990's he handled mass civil litigation in many states, was a board member and President of Concern America, an international aid organization, and relocated his law practice from San Francisco to Sonoma County. During the 1990's, Mr. Lanahan coordinated the LTryptophan liability litigation nationwide, resulting in the Japanese manufacturer indemnifying his 158 U.S. food supplement and vitamin industry clients for an amount in excess of $3 billion dollars.

He served on and chaired many for profit and nonprofit boards of directors including the North Bay Leadership Council, California Rural Broadcasting Corp. (KRCB) and the St. Joseph Health System of Sonoma County (Santa Rosa Memorial Hospital). Mr. Lanahan taught a course on Legendary Trials at Sonoma State University, Empire Law School and San Francisco Law School. In 2007 the Board of Trustees of the California State University bestowed on him a Honorary Doctor of Laws for his work at Sonoma State's Life Long Learning Program, Business School Advisory Board and acting as Co-chair of the campaign that raised funds to construct the Green Music Center concert hall and education facility. He and his wife Sue have been honored with a number of community service awards. They now spend much of their time in Puerto Vallarta Mexico.

Lightning Source UK Ltd.
Milton Keynes UK
UKHW011843210122
397550UK00007B/363/J